IDENTIFYING

THE ANTICHRIST

IDENTIFYING THE ANTICHRIST

Revealing Truths, Confronting Myths & Misconceptions

PAUL R. WILD

7710-T Cherry Park Drive, Suite 224

Houston, TX 77095

(281) 830-8724

http://www.WorldwidePublishingGroup.com

Printed in the United States of America

ISBN: 978-1-68411-858-8

TABLE OF CONTENTS

Acknowledgment

Thanks to my nephew, Jordan Hastings, and to Bill Tobin, Sheila Dailey, and Ed Cates for their feedback, which helped me to expand into new areas of discussion for this book. Special thanks to Mike Morrison for the many hours of collaboration over many years to elucidate the issues discussed herein. Extra special thanks to my wife, Christy, for her comments, support, and encouragement.

May this book be worthy of the Lord Jesus, who gives insight into and understanding of prophecy.

[10] And I fell at his feet to worship him. And he said unto me, See thou do it not: I am thy fellow servant, and of thy brethren that have the testimony of Jesus: worship God: **for the testimony of Jesus is the spirit of prophecy.**

Revelation 19:10*

*All Scripture references are from the King James Version (KJV) of the Bible.

Chapter 1

THE STATEMENT OF THE PROBLEM

Considering that the antichrist will be the most evil human to ever exist and the one who will do the most damage to humanity in general and Christians in particular, it is incumbent on the Body of Christ to discover who this man is before he ascends to full power and influence. Why? Since God gave us prophecy to help guide our way and affect the way we conduct our affairs, the primary purpose is for **preparation.** The more prepared we are spiritually, mentally, emotionally, physically, financially, and perhaps even martially, the more successfully we can weather the storm. God takes no pleasure in His people suffering needlessly; as Peter said in 1 Peter 3:17, "For it is better, if the will of God be so, that ye suffer for well doing, than for evil doing," or even for foolish doing, as in failing to heed our Father's warnings. Therefore, I hope to provide in this book the tools for Christians to identify this wicked man for the purpose of stimulating preparation in all the ways mentioned above before he takes over the world.

Whenever I read books or articles covering the topic of the antichrist, I check to see if the authors provide a name for whom they believe the antichrist is. I suspect that most people who are interested in prophecy do the same. If you are like me, then sadly I must inform you that I have no name to provide, because I have yet to see anyone on the world stage who fits the bill for the antichrist.

Speculation within the Body of Christ on the identification of the antichrist has been ongoing over the last two millennia. From the earliest days after Christ's ascension to heaven, the candidates have run the gamut from Nero, to any number of other Roman emperors, to various Popes, to various European kings, to various presidents of the United States (US). Protestant theologians after the Reformation focused on the Popes, but over time this focus has become less popular, such that the Protestants eventually enlarged their scope to include one or more US presidents, members of the British monarchy, and various European leaders, such as Hitler. This demonstrates the craziness of the shotgun approach for identifying who the reprobate is.

The prophet Daniel was told by his angelic visitor in Chapter 12 that "many shall run to and fro, and knowledge shall be increased," suggesting that as we come closer in time to the return of Jesus, we should be able to get more clarity on who the antichrist is, because our knowledge of prophecy should increase. After all, Jesus told us that we should be able to see the signs of His return, so it follows that we should be able to get a better handle on comparing the somewhat cryptic, ancient prophecies to modern events, thus leading to some "Aha! Eureka! Now I get it!" moments. As an example of comparing the ancient prophecies to modern events to gain an understanding of the prophecies, I proposed in my book, <u>Is the United States Mentioned in Bible Prophecy? With a Treatise on the Ezekiel 38 and Psalm 83 Wars,</u> that the four symbolical beasts of Daniel 7 have been attributed incorrectly to ancient nations instead of modern nations, specifically the Anglo-American Alliance (lion with eagle's wings); the Russians with their Turkish, Syrian, and Iranian allies (bear with three ribs in its mouth); the Asians (leopard with four wings and four heads); all leading up to the antichrist (lion/bear/leopard amalgamation), who is "diverse" from the others in that he is a hybrid. These modern nations, with their jockeying for power and their geographic locations, match the Daniel 7 narrative far better than the ancient nations proposed by most theologians, namely the Babylonians, Medo-Persians, Greeks, and Romans, thus giving illumination to what Daniel saw.

In the same vein, modern students of prophecy are looking at current events to see if these events give insight into the ancient prophecies about the antichrist. The rise of genetic engineering has fueled speculation that he might be a clone of a previous Bible personality or a genetically engineered super human, thus giving a literal meaning to Genesis 3:15 in that Satan will beget his physical seed, the antichrist, just as the Father begot His physical Seed, the Messiah. The emphasis on multiculturalism and ecumenism, not only within cultural Christianity (I say "cultural," because I suspect many of the people pushing this agenda are lost souls) but between religions, has caused many prophecy buffs to propose that the antichrist also will be multi-cultural and ecumenical. The current Pope is certainly setting the stage for a multicultural, ecumenical beast as he reaches out to Muslims, Jews, Hindus, Buddhists, and Mormons, as well as trying to mend fences between Catholics, Protestants, and Orthodox. But, "Can two walk together, except they be agreed?" (Amos 3:3) Not likely.

Alright, so, rather than pontificating more on how modern students of prophecy are interpreting prophecy in light of current events, let's just cut to the chase and discuss some of the candidates who are being proposed. For this exercise, I am defining "modern" as the 19th Century to now.

The "Son of Perdition," Judas Iscariot

We will begin with A.W. Pink, the great British theologian of the late 19th to mid-20th Centuries. His theory is that the antichrist will be a revivified or reincarnated Judas Iscariot. The basis of this theory is that both Judas Iscariot and the antichrist are termed "the son of perdition" in John 17:12 and 2 Thessalonians 2:3, respectively. "Perdition" in its archaic use meant "destruction," but in current vernacular it's just another name for hell.

The problem with this view is that Scripture teaches it is appointed unto men to die once, after which comes the judgment (Hebrews 9:27), with obvious exceptions where God revivified people in the Biblical narrative. I say revivified rather than resurrected, because resurrection is not only revivification but revivification into an eternal, glorified body. In the Biblical narrative, God always revivified people who were believers or who would become believers to bring glory to Himself and to further His purposes, something that will not be the case for the antichrist. Revivification never occurred to unbelievers in the Biblical narrative; remember this point for the discussion below about Nimrod. Furthermore, we shouldn't get too worked up over the "son of perdition" epithet. The Old Testament (OT) identifies several people as sons or children of Belial. Paul identifies Belial as Satan in 2 Corinthians 6:15, and Jesus in John 8:44 accused the Pharisees of being of their father, the devil. Most of humanity from the Fall to now have been children of destruction/hell/devil, so no special consideration should be given to Judas Iscariot for that pejorative.

Nimrod and the Nephilim

Another interesting but fringe proposition is that the antichrist will be a revivified or cloned Nimrod, considered by many, perhaps most, Bible scholars as the founder of all the pagan, pantheistic, ungodly religions after the Flood. The story here is that Nimrod's perfectly preserved body was found within the ruins of the ancient city of Uruk, from whence Iraq gets its name, the grave having been found beneath where the Euphrates once coursed. Allegedly, in 2003 German archaeologists found the tomb of Gilgamesh, the protagonist of the *Gilgamesh Flood Epic* (ancient Sumerian Flood myth) who is also equated by some with Nimrod, after which the US military took the body while there for the second Gulf War and whisked it away for top secret research; a competing story is that Turkish researchers found the body in Nimrud Mountain in Bitlis, Turkey.

Regarding the Iraqi story, the body was allegedly red-haired, gigantic in proportion, and of interest to the US military for producing super soldiers. Web-based stories on this theory usually show a photo of unknown origin portraying a red-haired male in a crypt or coffin, resplendent with a crown and other regalia. The Scriptural proof text cited by the Nimrod proponents is Revelation 17:8, which says, "The beast that thou sawest was, and is not; and shall ascend out of the bottomless pit, and go into perdition: and they that dwell on the earth shall wonder… when they behold the beast that was, and is not, and

6

yet is." The stories typically morph into claims of proof for the return of the Nephilim (variably translated as "giants," "fallen ones," or "violent ones"), or those half-human, half-fallen-angel giants of Genesis 6, based on Jesus's proclamation in Matthew 24:37 that the time leading up to His return will be "as the days of Noah were"; recall that in the days of Noah, giants roamed the earth. An alternate theory is that the antichrist may also be from among the satanically revivified race of the Nephilim rather than Nimrod himself.

Before we move on to other candidates for the antichrist, more should be said about Nimrod. Why is he so important to the Nimrod-is-the-antichrist theorists? Nimrod is described in Scripture as "a mighty hunter before the Lord." Some claim that he became a Nephilim through some unknown means, citing the phrase in Genesis 10:8 that "he **began** to be a mighty one in the earth," similar to the Nephilim who "**became** mighty men which were of old, men of renown" from Genesis 6:4. Jewish rabbis and modern theologians have suggested that the true meaning of "mighty hunter" is that he was a hunter of men standing against or opposing the Lord. If the Book of Jasher is to be believed, Nimrod tried to kill Abraham and did kill his brother Haran but was in turn killed by Esau; Jasher is a book with dubious provenance allegedly printed in Hebrew in 1613 that supposedly fills in missing parts of the Genesis narrative. Nimrod generally is believed to be the instigator of the Tower of Babel debacle that led to God's confusion of the languages.

He is hypothesized as the protagonist Gilgamesh in the *Epic of Gilgamesh*, an Akkadian and Sumerian flood myth that is a highly distorted, perverse version of the actual Biblical Flood story. Gilgamesh is a profane and evil man in the story and seeks to attain immortality.

Some commentators also equate Nimrod to Amraphel, one of the Mesopotamian kings who kidnapped Abraham's family and stole all his goods. Still others equate him to Enmerkar, a Sumerian king who allegedly built the Sumerian city of Uruk, a.k.a. Erech (Iraq), noting that the suffix *-kar* at the end of Enmerkar's name means "hunter."

Nevertheless, no matter what the source is regarding Nimrod's life, whether real or fanciful, he was a truly foul ruler and the first post-diluvian to engage in open rebellion against the Lord. He is thus etched in history as the prototype for all godless rulers to follow, with emphasis on the final ruler, the antichrist. More about Nimrod is stated at the back of this chapter under a section entitled *The Nimrod Conundrum* to avoid disrupting the flow of the main text, and more about Nimrod will be said in Chapter 7.

These stories about Nimrod and the Nephilim are usually accompanied by the Giant of Kandahar story, which is that US soldiers during a mission in the Kandahar province of Afghanistan were attacked by a 12-ft to 15-ft tall, 1200-lb, red-haired giant that lived in a cave and stank to high heaven. After spearing a soldier, as the story is told, the soldiers killed him and flew him away in a helicopter, allegedly for top secret research into his genome.

The Alien Conspiracy

Adding more to the complexity of identifying the antichrist is the meteoric rise across the spectrum of humanity of the belief in extraterrestrial aliens – the Greys, the Greens, the Anunnaki, the Reptilians, the Pleiadians, the Arcturians, and on and on and on. Do some simple internet and YouTube searches and see for yourself. While non-believers attribute these alien encounters with true aliens, select Christian prophecy authors and online theorists see this as demonic deception that Satan will use to deceive the nations, one theory being that when the antichrist arrives on the scene, these "aliens" will come forward to endorse him. It is instructive to note that when the observations of Satan worshippers who claim to have encountered demons and those who say they've encountered aliens are compared, the creatures both parties describe sound very much the same. The narrative the prophecy theorists promote is that the stories of human abductions and experimentation by aliens are real and that Satan is trying to understand human physiology and genetics in order to produce his "seed," specifically the seed mentioned in Genesis 3:15, and to revivify the Nephilim to wreak havoc during the Tribulation. Furthermore, the theorists postulate that these demonic entities will say something to the effect that they have been watching us for millennia and feel that now is the time to reveal their chosen one to lead us into the future and save us from destroying ourselves. The theorists see Jesus's warning of signs and wonders in the heavens from Matthew 24 and John's recording of signs and wonders in the heavens from Revelation as allusions to these demonic "aliens" and their activities.

The Turkish Hypothesis

I previously made mention of Turkey. Regarding Turkey, a new theory has surfaced over the last ten to fifteen years or so that the Gog and Magog of Ezekiel 38 and 39 are Turkish rather than Russian (the dominant theory), and that Turkey will be the birthplace of the antichrist. In this theory, the antichrist is Muslim and will have his headquarters in Mecca, which is proposed as the real location of the Mystery Babylon of Revelation. Following these lines of thought, Recep Erdogan, the current President, is identified as a candidate for the antichrist. Further to the Turkish proposition, some propose that Istanbul is the location of Mystery Babylon of Revelation 17:5 as opposed to the usual suspect, Rome, since Istanbul also allegedly has seven hills. Regarding those theories, Mecca, Istanbul, and Rome are incorrect candidates for the center of the antichrist's power, since Revelation 17:9-10 equate seven mountains to seven kings or kingdoms, not a geographic location. The proper place for the future Babylon the Great (Revelation 18:2,10,21) will be in Iraq, i.e., the "land of Shinar" of Zechariah 5:11. More on that later.

The Turkish Muslim proponents offer Revelation 13:18 as another piece of evidence.

[18] Here is wisdom. Let him that hath understanding count the number of the beast: for it is the number of a man; and his number is Six hundred threescore and six.

Revelation 13:18

They state that the original Greek text for Revelation 13:18 has the appearance of the Islamic basmala/bismillah creed in a corrupt Greek text, <u>Codex Vaticanus</u> (CV), which is an uncial (written in capital letters) manuscript from ~350 A.D. in the Vatican Library. The basmala creed is the Arabic باسم الله, meaning "In the name of God," with the full creed stated as bi-smi llāhi r-raḥmāni r-raḥīm, بِسْمِ اللهِ الرَّحْمٰنِ الرَّحِيْمِ, "In the name of God, the Most Gracious, the Most Merciful." The Arabic word for Allah is in the bold, underlined text above. The argument is made that the Greek text for 666 in the CV appears similar to the Arabic text for "the Name of Allah" in the basmala, followed by the Islamic symbol of two crossed swords for jihad, or holy war. The Greek letter chi is supposed to symbolize the two crossed swords. Furthermore, they argue that the English word "count" should be translated as "reckon" or "decide" and that the English word "number" should be translated as "multitude." Without further belaboring the details, their resultant translation roughly means that the antichrist can be identified through the multitudes that will follow him and who use the phrase "in the name of Allah and jihad."

Regarding the CV that the Turkish Muslim proponents use to make their argument, liberal scholars claim this manuscript is one of the "oldest and best" Greek manuscripts of the NT available, but the CV is corrupt because it omits large sections of Genesis, Psalms, and Hebrews; entirely omits Revelation and Paul's pastoral letters, such as 1 and 2 Timothy, which is against God's prohibition in Revelation 22:19 to not detract or subtract from His word; and includes the non-canonical Apocryphal books (e.g., Ecclesiasticus, Judith, Tobit), which is against God's prohibition in Revelation 22:18 to not add to His word. Revelation was added to the CV by an unknown person in the 15th Century using a miniscule (written in lower case Greek letters) text; therefore, the text used by the Turkish Muslim proponents to make their argument was not even part of the original CV. There are many other errors in the CV beyond these, very notably the absence of the Johannine Comma of 1 John 5:7-8 that is one of the strongest passages supporting Trinitarianism, indicating the first mistake of the basmala proponents was to cite the CV. The portion of the CV from Revelation 13:18 showing the Greek gematria for 666 is underlined below (https://digi.vatlib.it/view/MSS_Vat.gr.1209)

12

For those unfamiliar with gematria, it is a system in Hebrew and Greek in which letters equate to numbers.

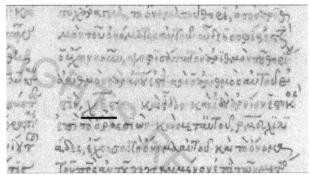

Revelation 13:18 Greek text from CV, Vat. Gr. 1209, p. 1530, 2019, Biblioteca Apostolica Vaticana (reproduced by permission, all rights reserved)

I consulted the Textus Receptus (TR, Received Text, as in the one received from God) to see another example of the Turkish Muslim proponents' miniscule 666 citation in a widely-accepted manuscript that is not corrupt (https://www.originalbibles.com).[1]

---

[1]The debate rages on between the KJV-only proponents who support the TR and the scholars of the liberal seminaries and denominations supporting the CV. The term "Textus Receptus" was not coined until 1633 when the Elzevir brothers published their version of the TR, which for all practical purposes refers to a body of texts compiled by Erasmus, Robert Estienne (a.k.a. Stephanus), and Beza. The TR forms the basis of the KJV, whereas the Revised Standard Version (RSV), New American Standard Bible (NASB), New International Version (NIV), and essentially all versions published after the Anglicans' 1881 English revision are based on corrupt Greek texts (e.g., CV and Sinaiticus Aleph) rather than the TR; the liberal scholars vigorously defend the corrupt texts. The New King James Version (NKJV) is based largely on the TR and is much closer in translation to the KJV than the others but still lets some errors from the corrupt versions slip in. Side-by-side comparisons of the newer versions to the KJV and NKJV show degradations of basic orthodoxy related to the deity of Jesus, such as 1 Timothy 3:16 wherein "God was manifest in the flesh" in the KJV is degraded in later versions by supplanting "God" with "He"; numerous deletions of words and entire verses are rampant in the later versions. Outright historical errors also occur in the later versions, such as in Hebrews 9:2-4 where the altar of incense is confused with the golden censer and is described as located within the Holy of Holies when it was not, thereby incorrectly describing the layout of the Tabernacle in the Wilderness. This author has studied extensively from the KJV, NKJV, NASB, RSV, and NIV and found the KJV far superior to later versions, although the NKJV can be useful if used with caution.

The TR is the basis of the KJV. The inspired Greek text is shown below, taken from Erasmus's 1516 TR and Beza's 1598 TR, with their respective Latin translations. Two examples are shown based on the principle of "In the mouth of two or three witnesses shall every word be established." (2 Corinthians 13:1)

Greek   Latin

Text of Greek NT compiled by Desiderius Erasmus Roterodamus with Latin translation

Greek   Latin

Text of Greek NT compiled by Theodore Beza with Latin translation

The underlined Greek text on the left is the Greek gematria 666, where the Greek letters chi (x), xi (ξ), and stigma (ς) equate to 600, 60, and 6, respectively.

There is more to refute their position. You will note underlined on the right of the TR texts the Latin words that translate as "compute (or count) the number of the beast." I have underlined the Latin word "numerus" three times which, when combined with the idea of computing or counting, emphasize that numbers are in mind here. It is evident that Erasmus and Beza believed that the gematria for 666 really did equate to a number, not an Arabic word for Allah. Context is everything.

More to that, how would a Greek-reading Christian of the 1st or 2nd Centuries know to apply the gematria for 666 to the god of a religion 500+ years in the future? How would the average Jew or Christian know to do it now? The written Word must have a plain meaning to the first readers as well as to us, even if neither group understands the prophetic meaning. With respect to translations of the original languages, I am leery of new translations that greatly deviate from generally accepted translations that have stood the test of time. This is to say that I reject the Turkish Muslim antichrist theorists' position and their translation of Revelation 13:18, though I believe Islam will be a component of the antichrist's background but not the full story, as will be explained in Chapter 11.

The British Royals

With the discussion of Turkey, we've moved west a bit out of the Middle East into Europe. We now need to work our way still further to the west to address a theory with a sizeable number of adherents, namely that the royals of England form the breeding pool from whence the antichrist arises. Charles has been the primary candidate, but because he's relatively old, his son, William, has become the new candidate. This theory was partially spawned from the British Israelism movement that was first proposed in the 1500's. This will be dealt with in more detail in following chapters, but suffice it to say that these folks believe a daughter of King Zedekiah escaped Babylonian captivity and sailed to the British Isles to become the progenitor of the Irish, British, Scottish, and Welsh kings. Thus, the claim is made that the royals are descendants of King David, allowing the alleged antichrist King of England to lay claim to the throne of Israel. The royals are frequently cited by conspiracy theorists as being associated with the thirteen Illuminati bloodlines, and the Merovingians, and the Black Nobility, and the Freemasons, and whatever else; these groups allegedly also include the Rothschilds, the Du Ponts, the Rockefellers, etc., who are purported to be Luciferians behind the push for a one-world government. Borrowing from my book, The Timing of the Rapture, below is a summary of points about the royals that the British monarchy proponents cite:

Another view that has gained traction in some circles is that the antichrist is Prince Charles of Wales or his son, William. They make their case based on several points, such as Charles is a literal prince; he claims to be descended from King David; he is part Greek through his father and therefore descended from one of the ancient kingdoms that will comprise part of the antichrist's kingdom; England was part of the Roman empire, thus making him of the "people of the prince who is to come"; he has embraced Islam to some extent (thus rejecting the God of his fathers); he defines himself as "the defender of faith" rather than "the defender of **the** faith (Christianity)," the moniker that his predecessors used; he claims to have had a revelatory, mystical experience in the late 1970's that redefined his mission in life; his coat of arms contains a red dragon, ten lions (heraldic beasts), and other symbols that seemingly have Biblical corollaries; and he has aligned himself with the power brokers of the EU.

Again, we need to concentrate on the Scriptures at hand rather than an unsubstantiated lineage to David or other conspiratorial claims. Maybe the conspiracy folks are right about some of their claims, but I don't put much stock in the monarchy-as-antichrist angle, for reasons elucidated later.

A Cornucopia of Candidates

Regarding other candidates who have received mention over the last 40 to 50 years, I'll simply list them:

- Whichever Pope holds the office, currently Pope Francis

- Lord Maitreya, a man who allegedly revealed himself to be the Buddha/Christ/Mahdi at a 2009 conference in London and promoted by New Age promoter Benjamin Creme

- Ronald Reagan

- Henry Kissinger

- Boutros Boutros-Ghali

- Mikhail Gorbachev

- Bill Gates

- Bill Clinton

- Barack Obama

- Vladimir Putin

- Emmanuel Macron

- Jared Kushner

- George H.W. Bush – he has been given dishonorable mention as a previous candidate by some prophecy speculators because of his "new world order" comment in one of his speeches

No doubt there are others, but these are just the ones I know of. As with many of the prospects for the antichrist down through the ages, the inclusions of the above-referenced men on the list have been based more on their perceived wickedness and access to power than on consistency with attributes of the antichrist described in Scripture. Some are on the list because someone used the Greek and/or Hebrew gematria to calculate the number of their names and apparently came up with 666 as the value of their names. In any case, the Body of Christ needs to move away from this sloppy approach and use Scripture as the lens through which we see the antichrist.

Satan's Seed

Finally, I would be remiss if I did not introduce a new theory, at least new to me, and one in which I must give credit to my good friend, Michael Morrison. Mike is frequently my sounding board for exploring various doctrines, tenets of the faith, and theories on various issues of prophecy, and we have spent hundreds of hours examining Scripture, particularly those passages of the prophetic type, from various angles. Mike suggested that the following verse be taken quite literally rather than figuratively; the Church has taken the figurative approach the last two millennia.

[15] And I will put enmity between thee and the woman, and between thy seed and her seed; it shall bruise thy head, and thou shalt bruise his heel.

Genesis 3:15

Mike suggested employing a straight-forward approach to interpreting Satan's "seed." I would liken this to employing Occam's razor, the theory that the simplest solution to a problem is usually the correct one. If the Father intended to bring forth His Son through the seed of a woman, as conceived by the Holy Spirit, then why not interpret the verse literally that Satan will spawn a child of his own body in the same way that the "sons of God," i.e., fallen angels, of Genesis 6 did in their liaisons with "daughters of men" to produce the giant Nephilim? Instead of going down a rabbit hole that will slow down our progress, I think it is better to reserve this theory for a standalone discussion entitled *Satanic Sexuality* that is presented after *The Nimrod Conundrum* at the back of this chapter.

A Proposed Description

I want to reiterate that I can't give a name for the antichrist, but I will take a crack at describing him according to appearance, race, ethnicity, culture, birthplace, and personality, among other attributes. My theory for his description is based on Scriptural references that are cited in subsequent chapters, but I think it is best to place the

20

description right up front to avoid frustrating the reader by dragging it out. That being said, it is now time to describe him. Here goes:

I believe the antichrist could be described as…

…exceptionally handsome, physically imposing, 30 years old, brilliant, skilled communicator; multicultural, black or dark-skinned Jew of the Tribe of Dan from Iraq; of Muslim upbringing and Christian cultural influence; with no regard for what women think, want, or hold in high esteem; and **utterly evil**.

In the following 14 chapters, I will present the Scriptural evidence for these attributes. My hope is to provide the Body of Christ a description accurate enough to help watchful members of the Body identify the antichrist before he ascends to power, the end goal being to spur the Body into preparation for the coming storm. This is in line with something that has been burning in me for many years, which is to wake the Church up, and in line with the wisdom described by Solomon, to wit:

[3] A prudent man foreseeth the evil, and hideth himself: but the simple pass on, and are punished.

Proverbs 22:3

The Nimrod Conundrum

The Nimrod-Nephilim connection requires further investigation. It hinges on understanding a verse that has given fits to theologians for generations.

> 8 The beast that thou sawest was, and is not; and shall ascend out of the bottomless pit, and go into perdition: and they that dwell on the earth shall wonder, whose names were not written in the book of life from the foundation of the world, when they behold the beast that was, and is not, and yet is.
>
> Revelation 17:8

How can you have a being that existed once, does not exist now, and yet will ascend out of hell to exist again, only to be cast into hell once more? The Nimrod-is-the-antichrist theorists claim the key to understanding the Nimrod conundrum is understanding the relationship of Nimrod to the Nephilim. The points of connection between Nimrod and the Nephilim are exceptionally strange, so hold on for a wild ride.

We will begin with the Nephilim, but before plowing into them, we must first resolve the issue of whether they are (1) children of fallen angels and women or (2) children of women of the ungodly line of Cain and men of the godly line of Seth, Adam's first and third sons, respectively. I am squarely in the fallen angel-women camp, since the "sons of God" term used in Genesis 6:1-4 is, with one exception, used only in the OT to describe beings that originated directly from God without human involvement through natural birth, Adam being one of them (Luke 3:38) and the others being the angelic host. The exception in the OT is that the term is used in Hosea 1:10 to describe the redeemed Israelites **after** their acceptance of Jesus as Messiah just before and during His Millennial reign. In that way, they become sons of God in the way that all Christians become sons of God, as the first verse of the New Testament (NT) that uses that term, John 1:12, indicates:

> [12] But as many as received him, to them gave he power to become the sons of God [you see, we **become** the sons of God through faith in Jesus], even to them that believe on his name:

John 1:12

The fallen angel-women approach then gives illumination to the strange phrase in Genesis 6:9, that "Noah...was perfect in his generations." This means he was a pure-blood, untainted by Nephilim DNA, and not a reference to his high moral character, although he is called a "just man" in Genesis 6:9. Should anyone want to contest my position, I recommend finding Chuck Missler's teachings on the issue through his YouTube videos or on the Koinonia House web site, since I don't want to get bogged down and sidetracked from the main topic of this section.

Returning to the main topic, a relatively new theory has been proposed by various non-mainstream students of prophecy, meaning those who are not products of the Protestant seminaries, Protestant denominational leadership, or Protestant mega-churches, that the demons of the NT that Jesus encountered were not fallen angels in league with Satan but rather the disembodied spirits of Nephilim. No offense intended against the Roman Catholic and Orthodox factions, but they don't seem to have as much interest in apocalyptic studies as the Protestants, so I feel that the bulk of the adherents of this new theory are Protestants. In any case, this theory is slowly gaining more wide-spread acceptance in the Body of Christ. Assuming that the bulk of my reading audience came from a traditional church background of Roman Catholic, Protestant, or Orthodox origin, it is likely that the demons described in Sunday school, from the pulpit, and in Christian literature were defined as fallen angels; therefore, the concept of disembodied Nephilim being the demons of the NT would be a very foreign concept to Roman Catholics, Protestants, and Orthodox taught in old-school orthodoxy.

Under this new theory, the 2,000 demons of Matthew 8, Mark 5, and Luke 8 that Jesus cast out of the possessed men and into a herd of pigs were disembodied Nephilim, not fallen angels. Remember that Jesus said in Luke 11:24-26 that the demons seek to inhabit people rather than wander the "dry places," a euphemism for hell. Contrast that to the fallen angel "stars of heaven" of Revelation 12:4 and the "sons of God" who appeared before God – Satan being one of them – of Job 1:6, 2:11, and 38:7. Satan is a fallen angel whom Paul calls "the prince of the power of the air"; he and his fellow fallen angels do not wander the dry places seeking to inhabit humans but still have access to the throne room of God, as Job 1 and Revelation 12:3-10 indicate. It's a bizarre thought, yet true, that the demons and fallen angels inhabit different realms and have different functions, yet all of it for nefarious purposes.

The next step in evaluating the Nimrod-is-the-antichrist theory is to deal with the theology of the origin of the human spirit. Isaiah says the following:

> 5 Thus saith God the Lord, he that created the heavens, and stretched them out; he that spread forth the earth, and that which cometh out of it; **he that giveth breath unto the people upon it, and spirit to them that walk therein**:
>
> Isaiah 42:5

Zechariah says:

> 1The burden of the word of the Lord for Israel, saith the Lord, which stretcheth forth the heavens, and layeth the foundation of the earth, and **formeth the spirit of man within him**.
>
> Zechariah 12:1

And Hebrews says:

> [9]Furthermore we have had fathers of our flesh which corrected us, and we gave them reverence: shall we not much rather be in subjection unto the **Father of spirits,** and live?

Hebrews 12:9

What is the significance of this? Simply put, if Nimrod's body or a Nephilim body were to be revivified through cloning or some other demonic, genetic manipulation to become the antichrist, it would mean that God would have to put a spirit within him, which seems utterly preposterous, and it would seem to violate the passage from Hebrews 9:27 that says humans only die once and after that comes judgment. Remember from the discussion above that Scripture records that only believers were revivified, never unbelievers. Perhaps God will allow one exception to Hebrews 9:27 and permit Satan to bring Nimrod's spirit out of hell, since God frequently allowed Satan to do outrageous things, only to use Satan's actions against God to bring glory to Himself and to further His purposes. If you don't believe me, then I invite you to read the book of Job.

Make no mistake about it, the spirit of the original Nimrod is suffering in hell, just as all other lost souls are, or is wandering between earth and hell, if the alternate theory proposed by some is true that Nimrod's spirit was altered into a demonic Nephilim spirit as he "began to be a mighty one in the earth." If God allows no exceptions to Hebrews 9:27 (people die once, then judgment) for unbelievers and no exceptions to the accompanying prohibition against unbelievers being revivified, then the Nimrod-is-the-antichrist theorists must find another explanation for how the body of Nimrod gets a spirit to live because, recall, James 2:26 says, "...the body without the spirit is dead..." How can you provide a revivified Nimrod body which cannot be revivified spiritually for the reasons stated above, but provide a spirit in order to live, because James 2:26 says human flesh must have a spirit to live? You do it by possessing that body with a disembodied Nephilim, i.e., a demon.

If my proposition is true that the antichrist will be born of a Jewish woman (see Chapter 8), and if the Nimrod-is-the-antichrist theorists' position is true that the antichrist is Satan's seed through genetic manipulation, then logically it leads to the conclusion that a Jewish woman will have to be impregnated by other than human means to bear the antichrist. A strange thought, yet not beyond the delusional schemes of the enemy.

The idea of a surrogate mother for the antichrist is not novel, for even Hollywood took that approach back in the 1970's with *The Omen*, a movie starring Gregory Peck in which the antichrist is born of a jackal. This is an early form of "predictive programming," the phenomenon wherein Hollywood, functioning as a tool of Satan, presents satanic concepts, such as genetically modified super humans and aliens, to acclimate us and prepare us to accept deception.

Add to the mind-blowing concept of the Jewish surrogate mother the theory that the selected Jewish woman will be married to a Muslim man (see Chapter 11), who will not be the biological father. What if the Jewish woman is a virgin still untouched by her Muslim husband? What if a hellish creature disguised as an angel of light makes proclamation to this deceived couple of the coming Messiah/Mahdi? Can you see where this could lead? Can you see the possibility of mimicry and mockery by Satan of the method used by the Father to bring the Son into the world? In this manner, the antichrist could falsely claim divine origin and, in one more way, attempt to duplicate the plans of God for the purpose of deceiving humanity. Bizarre, crazy, outlandish, but absolutely in line with the perverse ways of the serpent.

Let's summarize: the Nimrod-is-the-antichrist theorists claim that Nimrod's body or a Nephilim body will be revivified with modern technology and indwelled either by Nimrod's spirit or by a disembodied, Nephilim demon, thereby fulfilling the prophecy of Revelation 17:8. In this manner, the antichrist would then touch all the points of that verse, that (1) he is the beast that was, meaning he existed in a time before the Apostle John's time, (2) he is not, meaning he did not exist in John's time and does not exist now, (3) he will ascend out of hell by way of his spirit being released from hell or possessed by a demon coming from that domain, and (4) he will again suffer the fires of hell. In this way, it literally could be said of the antichrist that he is the seed of Satan and the son of perdition. I can't say that I endorse these theories; nevertheless, since Jesus said things will get exceptionally weird just before He returns, neither can I say that I dismiss these theories. Still, I think it is better to focus on what Scripture says about the antichrist, as I do in following chapters, rather than tenuous, unsubstantiated claims.

Satanic Sexuality

If you were to explore the topic of the sexual interactions of the angelic host with women by going online to do various internet and YouTube word searches, you would be overwhelmed with the websites and accounts that deal with this topic. Conventional books from conventional publishers covering this issue, combined with blogs, websites, and YouTube channels, are available by the reams. If you explore the topic long enough, eventually you will encounter the theory that the real story behind the Garden of Eden forbidden fruit account is not one of eating the fruit but of a sexual encounter between Eve and the serpent, i.e., Satan. The proponents of the Eve-Satan tryst say that Satan "beguiled" Eve (2 Corinthians 11:3), applying a sexual connotation to the word when it simply means "tricked," as it obviously means in other passages of Scripture (e.g., Joshua 9:22) where no sexual connotation can be construed. The proponents then posit that

Cain was the fruit of that encounter. I would say that these people violate the Occam's razor principle cited previously in that they highly contort the direct statements that Adam and Eve ate a piece of fruit from a tree that God said was *verboten*. They would argue that Adam stood idly by while this tryst occurred, since the Biblical narrative clearly indicates that Adam was there when Satan deceived Eve. Silly. Allegorizing run amok.

We can ignore the Satan-Eve liaison theory as a figment of some very creative imaginations, but we cannot ignore the Genesis 6 narrative of the liaisons of fallen angels with women, since Scripture simply states it plainly.

> [1] And it came to pass, when men began to multiply on the face of the earth, and daughters were born unto them, [2] That the sons of God saw the daughters of men that they were fair; and they took them wives of all which they chose. [3] And the Lord said, My spirit shall not always strive with man, for that he also is flesh: yet his days shall be an hundred and twenty years. [4] There were giants [Hebrew *Nephilim*] in the earth in those days; and also after that, when the sons of God came in unto the daughters of men, and they bare children to them, the same became mighty men which were of old, men of renown.
>
> Genesis 6:1-4

If you continue your research into satanic sexuality, you will discover that many, many students of this topic are firmly convinced that the fallen angels and Nephilim form the basis of the Greek, Roman, Egyptian, Indian, and Norse god and demi-god mythologies, as well as those of other ancient cultures. In their minds, when Odysseus (Ulysses) had his run-in with the cyclops in Homer's <u>Odyssey</u>, Homer may well have meant that a literal giant with one eye once existed. The stories of the Titans and their war against the gods are viewed as romanticized versions of actual events carried down over time through oral transmission until someone finally recorded them.

It is not without a Biblical basis that these theorists make their claims. They cite the extra-Biblical but Biblically-endorsed <u>Book of Enoch</u>, referencing the following passages as proof that at least some portions of this non-canonical book are historically accurate, since the Apostle Peter and Jude the half-brother of Jesus reference it.

> [4] For if God spared not the angels that sinned, but cast them down to hell, and delivered them into chains of darkness, to be reserved unto judgment; [9] The Lord knoweth how to deliver the godly out of temptations, and to reserve the unjust unto the day of judgment to be punished:
>
> 2 Peter 2:4,9

⁶ And the angels which kept not their first estate, but left their own habitation, he hath reserved in everlasting chains under darkness unto the judgment of the great day. ⁷ Even as Sodom and Gomorrha, and the cities about them in like manner, giving themselves over to fornication, and going after strange flesh, are set forth for an example, suffering the vengeance of eternal fire. ⁸ Likewise also these filthy dreamers defile the flesh, despise dominion, and speak evil of dignities. ¹⁴ And Enoch also, the seventh from Adam, prophesied of these, saying, Behold, the Lord cometh with ten thousands of his saints, ¹⁵ To execute judgment upon all, and to convince all that are ungodly among them of all their ungodly deeds which they have ungodly committed, and of all their hard speeches which ungodly sinners have spoken against him.

Jude 6-8,14-15

Enoch describes in detail 200 fallen angels intermingling with women to produce the Nephilim and the resultant fallout leading to the Flood. Peter does not reference Enoch directly but rather indirectly, because the canonical OT that he had at his disposal does not describe the fate of the fallen angels who intermingled with women in the way that Enoch does, specifically in Chapters 53 and 54. Also, Peter indirectly references Enoch by referring to "chains of darkness," similar to Jude's "chains under darkness," and Jude directly ascribes historical veracity to <u>Enoch</u> by referencing "Enoch also, the seventh from Adam..." (Jude 14) Peter states that the angels "sinned." Jude tells us how they sinned – sexually – for he indicates that the angels did not remain in the state that God had created for them but pursued sexual gratification, "even as Sodom and Gomorrha" did. Logic dictates that they must have done something very egregious to be confined to a place that the rest of their fallen angelic brethren are not now confined to, since one-third of the angelic host will not lose their current residency in the heavenly realm until Satan gathers them up and casts them to earth when he finally is thrown out of heaven (Revelation 12:4,9).

Many scholars now believe that Peter, Jude, and their compatriots ascribed historical validity to <u>Enoch,</u> even though it is not considered canonical nor worthy of final authority in matters of Christian orthodoxy. Not a problem – an ancient book that is not part of Scripture should not be construed as having no historical accuracy, for if that were the case, we would have to ignore the works of Josephus, Herodotus, Tacitus, Manetho, ad infinitum. <u>Enoch</u> is consistent with the OT in that the OT plainly records the races of the giants with names such as the Anakim and the Rephaim, in addition to the Nephilim. The 12 spies sent from Moses into Canaan said the giants were as tall as cedar trees and that the spies seemed like grasshoppers in comparison. King Og of Bashan and Goliath of the Philistines were giants.

Enoch records and is supported by Peter and Jude that the 200 fallen angels are consigned to the lowermost portions of hell until the final judgment, which I interpret to mean the Great White Throne judgment of Revelation 20:11 in which all accounts are paid in full and settled for all eternity for all beings, whether angelic, demonic, or human. What is the significance of this for our discussion on Satan's seed and satanic sexuality? For one thing, it provides another nail in the coffin of the silly theory that Satan violated Eve, for had he done that, he would have suffered the same fate as those fallen angels who did cavort with women. Stated plainly, he would have been tossed into the brig, yet he is not in the brig and is free to roam the earth.

But what if Satan, in a Hail Mary, last-ditch effort germinated in his self-deceived mind, with the knowledge of his inevitable fate at the end of Tribulation (he can read Scripture, too, you know, as demonstrated by his temptation of Jesus during His 40-day wilderness test), made a final attempt to thwart God's plan by doing what the Genesis 6 fallen angels did? What would he have to lose, since he knows he already has lost everything and is simply waiting for God's other shoe to drop? What if God was being utterly literal in His Genesis 3:15 statement to Satan, that Satan would produce his own seed to engage in a losing war with God's Seed? Even more so than the revivified Nimrod/Nephilim-Jewish woman hypothesis of the previous section, the antichrist could falsely claim divine

34

origin and, in one more way, more closely adhere to the virgin birth story of Christ's first advent in an attempt to duplicate the plans of God for the purpose of deceiving humanity. Well, this theory is more in keeping with our Occam's razor discussion and far more simplistic than the Nimrod/Nephilim-Jewish woman angle stated above. Wouldn't it be mind-blowing if the one idea for the antichrist's origin that seems the most outrageous is the correct one? A difficult idea to wrap your head around, yet not without some Scriptural support.

Identifying The Antichrist

Chapter 2

EXCEPTIONALLY HANDSOME

Since the world worships physical appearance far above spiritual integrity, logic suggests that Satan will have a far better chance of sucking lost souls into his deception if his boy looks really, really good. (This immediately disqualifies Charles, Recep, and Vladimir, but perhaps William, Emmanuel, and Jared might get in under the wire.) But the challenge here is to provide a Scriptural basis for my supposition, so I present the following.

> [1] Who hath believed our report? And to whom is the arm of the Lord revealed? [2] For he shall grow up before him as a tender plant, and as a root out of a dry ground: he hath no form nor comeliness; and when we shall see him, there is no beauty that we should desire him.
>
> Isaiah 53:1-2

Recent discoveries using 3-dimensional modeling of the Shroud of Turin support the prophecy that Jesus would not be selected for the cover of *GQ* magazine were He in His human form today. As a scientist, I firmly believe that there is an overwhelming amount of scientific data and provenance for the shroud demonstrating that the relic could not have been concocted by medieval artists and is indeed the burial shroud of Jesus. I utterly reject the naysayers' weak, so-called evidence against it, but it would not serve my purpose to dive into that here. Sufficient for now is to say that the 3-D modeled face staring back at us from the computer screen is not that of a suave, debonair model or movie star but that of the average man. Let us now further consider "there is no beauty that we should desire him." God employs the principle of opposites in his dealing with humanity, for He distances Himself from the ways of man, which are corrupt, profane, deceptive. The older shall serve the younger; the first shall be last and the last shall be first; the foolish are chosen to shame the wise; the Lord of Glory was born in a manger; the Creator was nailed to His created tree. You see, the antichrist is the **anti-Christ**. Excepting some characteristics of his that will be addressed in the following chapters, with respect to his personality, presentation, and appearance, he will be everything Jesus in His humanity was not.

Chapter 3

PHYSICALLY IMPOSING

Exceptionally handsome and physically imposing need not be mutually exclusive. In fact, many would say they go hand-in-hand and portray the ultimate in masculinity. Perhaps "ruggedly handsome" is the correct term. But where might the idea of this aspect of the antichrist originate? The following passages provide this tidbit about the antichrist.

> 20 And of the ten horns that were in his head, and of the other which came up, and before whom three fell; even of that horn that had eyes, and a mouth that spake very great things, whose look was **more stout** than his fellows.
>
> Daniel 7:20

²³ And in the latter time of their kingdom, when the transgressors are come to the full, a king of **fierce countenance**, and understanding dark sentences, shall stand up.

Daniel 8:23

So, we have a man who has a fierce countenance and is more stout than his associates. Let's address the stout aspect first.

Consulting the Hebrew text and its translation, we find that the Hebrew word for "stout" in Daniel 7:20 is *rab*. *Rab* most often is translated elsewhere in the OT as "great." *Rab* is used to describe a "great image" in Daniel 2:31 and a "great mountain" in Daniel 2:35, and it obviously is intended to transmit the idea of "large." This dovetails well with the next word, "fierce," in our discussion.

Now, turning our attention to the fierce aspect, we find that the Hebrew word for "fierce" in Daniel 8:23 is *az*. *Az* frequently is translated elsewhere in the OT as strong or mighty. I feel relatively safe in saying that most people would ascribe large physical size and muscularity to these descriptors. Some in the reading audience may recall the late Franco Columbu, the great Italian body builder and strongman of the 1970s and 1980s, who was only 5 feet 5 inches tall yet could deadlift nearly 800 pounds. Although very muscular and strong, he cannot capture the imagination of size and strength anywhere near the level of

40

someone like Hafþór Júlíus Björnsson, the winner of the 2018 World's Strongest Man competition who also plays the part of Gregor "The Mountain" Clegane in the HBO series, *Game of Thrones*. At 6 feet 9 inches tall and over 400 pounds, I doubt anyone on the planet would say he does not have a fierce countenance, or appearance, if you will. I'm suggesting that the antichrist will have a comparable appearance, or even more so.

Those who postulate that the antichrist may be a revivified Nephilim or some other supersized genetic freak of sorts may well find comfort in these two passages as support for their theories. Irrespective of the various theories on the origin of the antichrist, it is clear that he will be physically imposing in some way, shape, or form. He will stand out from his associates, whoever they may be, like a sore thumb. I would add that this feature alone would immediately eliminate all the existing candidates for the antichrist mentioned in Chapter 1.

Chapter 4

THIRTY YEARS OLD

I can find no definitive proof that the antichrist will be 30 years of age when he ascends to power, but considering that Satan will try to counterfeit Jesus in as many ways as he can, I believe it is probable that the antichrist will be that age at his epiphany. The rationale for this theory is based on the following:

> 23 And Jesus himself began to be about **thirty years of age**, being (as was supposed) the son of Joseph, which was the son of Heli,
>
> Luke 3:23

Thirty was the minimum age that a man from the Tribe of Levi could serve as a priest.

> 46 All those that were numbered of the Levites, whom Moses and Aaron and the chief of Israel numbered, after their families, and after the house of their fathers, 47 From

thirty years old and upward even unto fifty years old, every one that came to do the service of the ministry, and the service of the burden in the tabernacle of the congregation.

Numbers 4:46-47

As Paul informs us in Hebrews 2:17 and 4:14, Jesus was and is our faithful and great High Priest. Since Jesus said in Matthew 5:17 that He came not to destroy the Law but to fulfill the Law, it was necessary for Him to be at least the age of 30 to begin His ministry as our faithful and great High Priest to lead us to our Father God. Likewise, under the assumption that the antichrist will seek legitimacy from his Jewish brethren, he will need to be at least 30 years old to function in his capacity as a demonic high priest to lead the lost to his father, Satan.

On a practical basis, what are the ramifications of this age limit? When will he arrive on the scene? Is he alive now? This is sheer speculation on my part, but I suspect that he might be only a child at this time. My reasoning for this is based on the chronology of Daniel 7 coupled with Ezekiel 38-39. Daniel 7 prophesies that the US and probably England (lion with eagle's wings) must first be judged; then the Russians with their Turkish, Syrian, and Iranian allies (bear with three ribs in its mouth); and finally the Asians (leopard with four heads and four wings). I suspect that the US perhaps has one, two, or at most three more presidential election cycle(s) before it

44

implodes, allowing the Russians (Gog and Magog) and their Muslim allies of Ezekiel 38-39 and the Muslims of Psalm 83 to invade Israel and subsequently be destroyed. Ezekiel 39 says that the invading Ruso-Muslim hordes' weapons will be burned for seven years, suggesting that the antichrist will not yet have invaded Israel during that period. Somewhere along the way the Asian beast must be defeated, and probably quickly if it follows the patterns of the American and Russian beasts, allowing the final beast to absorb all the predecessor beasts' kingdoms. If we stack these events back-to-back-to-back, I postulate that we have another 15 to 25 years or so before the antichrist ascends to power, and certainly not less than 10 years. If so, then he would be a pre-teen child to perhaps a teenager at this time. Adulthood can come more quickly than we think; therefore, time is of the essence for the Body to prepare for his arrival.

Chapter 5

BRILLIANT, SKILLED COMMUNICATOR

I hate to say this, but there will be some characteristics of the beast that will be very much like Jesus, specifically brilliant and fluid of speech, yet with a perverse, profane twist. The following verses describe the situation.

> 23 And in the latter time of their kingdom, when the transgressors are come to the full, a king of fierce countenance, and understanding **dark sentences**, shall stand up. 24 And his power shall be mighty, but not by his own power: and he shall destroy wonderfully, and shall prosper, and practise, and shall destroy the mighty and the holy people. 25 And through his policy also he shall cause **craft** to prosper in his hand; and he shall magnify himself in his heart, and by peace shall destroy many: he shall also stand up against the Prince of princes; but he shall be broken without hand.

> Daniel 8:23-25

Let's break it down.

"…understanding dark sentences…": "Lemma" is the term used by linguists for the root word in Hebrew, Greek, and other languages that serves as the basis for various forms of a word according to tense, mood, case, gender, and number, depending on whether the word is a verb or a noun. In this case, the Hebrew lemma for "dark sentences" is *chidah,* and its derivations are used variably in Scripture to refer to riddles, perplexing words, proverbs, parables, and dark sayings or sentences. Therefore, we can deduce that this beast will have to be intellectually brilliant to be able to understand these perplexing things, whatever they may be.

"…he shall cause craft to prosper…": The Hebrew lemma *sekel* and its derivations are used variably in Scripture to refer to insight, understanding, wisdom, prudence, or cunning. It is perhaps this last synonym, cunning, that is most apropos, for it links the previous synonyms to the idea of deception. Indeed, one definition of cunning that I found on the internet describes it as "having or showing skill in achieving one's ends by deceit or evasion." Regarding his skill as a communicator, I originally was going to use "orator" as a descriptor, but I thought it was too much of a stretch. I suspect that he will be a great orator, along the lines of an Adolf Hitler, but perhaps not, for one can be a great communicator without being electrifying in delivery. Nevertheless, a brilliant mind coupled with eloquent but deceptive speech is required to be able to deceive the bulk of the earth's people. You'd have to be a very tricky person to lull the nations, most pointedly Israel, into thinking peace is your objective when it is exactly the opposite.

Chapter 6

MULTICULTURAL

⁷ After this I saw in the night visions, and behold a fourth beast, dreadful and terrible, and strong exceedingly; and it had great iron teeth: it devoured and brake in pieces, and stamped the residue with the feet of it: and it was diverse from all the beasts that were before it; and it had **ten horns**.

Daniel 7:7

¹ And I stood upon the sand of the sea, and saw a beast rise up out of the sea, having seven heads and **ten horns**, and upon his horns ten crowns, and upon his heads the name of blasphemy. ² And the beast which I saw was like unto a leopard, and his feet were as the feet of a bear, and his mouth as the mouth of a lion: and the dragon gave him his power, and his seat, and great authority.

Revelation 13:1-2

This beast of Daniel 7 is the same beast as the one in Revelation 13. Reading all of Daniel 7 and then connecting the dots to Revelation 13:2, you will see that the fourth beast of Daniel 7 is an amalgamation of the three predecessor beasts, being part lion, part bear, and part leopard of western, northern, and eastern regions of the earth, respectively. I highlighted **ten horns** to show the connection between the passages. The primary descriptor of the Revelation 13:2 beast is the leopard, an animal with a yellow coat, black spots, and white underbelly. This animal is both Asian and African and was once common in the Middle East, including Israel. As a child, I recall reading in the World Book Encyclopedia that humanity is composed of three primary races, specifically the Caucasoids (whites), Negroids (blacks), and Mongoloids (yellows, or those folks hailing from the Mongols, i.e., Asiatics). Modern anthropologists do not strictly adhere to these classifications and consider them antiquated; nonetheless, laymen still see through these three lenses.

One commenter commenting on a YouTube video lesson taught by a pastor covering this topic called these concepts "disgusting stereotypes," but I would reply, "Nonsense," and counter that stereotypes exist for a reason in that they conveniently and often accurately describe large groups of people, places, and things. The Bible is not politically correct, nor should we be. We are called sheep in Scripture, deservedly I might add, since humanity's behavior has been much akin to those silly, easily lost, easily captured and killed animals. The stereotype fits. Therefore, the use of a leopard is a simplistic but fitting way for God to identify a characteristic of the beast for silly, sheep-like humans, that he will be appealing to all the cultures (and races) of humanity. Beyond that, it also suggests that he will hail from Asiatic and/or African regions, as you will see in the following chapter.

.

Chapter 7

BLACK OR DARK SKINNED

[23] Can the Ethiopian change his skin, or the leopard his spots? then may ye also do good, that are accustomed to do evil.

Jeremiah 13:23

The above-referenced verse is viewed by some students of prophecy as a key to assist in unlocking the mystery of the racial background of the antichrist, with one theory gaining momentum that he will be black or dark skinned. The leopard in Jeremiah 13:23 is linked by some theorists to the leopard in Revelation 13, which refers to the antichrist, and the leopard has black spots and is most commonly associated with Africa, just as an Ethiopian is, according to their theory. (But I would also point out that the leopard is also linked to Asia, which includes all countries east of the Mediterranean Sea, including Israel and its Muslim neighbors, like Iraq.) The Ethiopian is linked to Nimrod in that Ethiopians and Nimrod have a common lineage, and the antichrist is linked to Nimrod, as will be explained further below.

Admittedly, the idea that the antichrist is described in Scripture as racially black or dark skinned is a stretch, but there is a rationale to it. There are some scholars and students of prophecy who believe the antichrist is the fulfillment of a typology presented in the OT as Nimrod, the first world ruler and progenitor of all the anti-god, pantheistic religions that have infested the planet after the Flood. Note that he founded Babel, from whence we get the word for a confusing form of speech and the area of the world called Babylon; bear this geographic location in mind for later discussion. Nimrod is an epithet rather than a formal name and, according to many commentators, means "the rebel," from the Hebrew verb *marad*, meaning "to rebel." Place the Hebrew letter *nun* with the vowel point *hiriq* for the "i" sound in "pit" in front of *marad* and you get the infinitive construct Nimrod: **The Rebel**.

Another approach taken by some to Nimrod's name is that it is a construct of the Hebrew *nmr* for leopard plus Hebrew *rad* for ruler, subduer, or conqueror, as in *Elrad* or *Elrod* – God rules - thereby making him the "leopard conqueror." Some commentators link Nimrod to the Egyptian god Osiris, associating Nimrod to images and statuary of Osiris wearing leopard clothing. Osiris is presented in ancient Egyptian art as green or black skinned. Osiris comes from the Greek transliteration from Egyptian phonetic *wsr*, or "mighty one" as one commentator argues, which then hearkens back to Nimrod being a "mighty hunter" of the Biblical record; the Hebrew word *gibbor* for "mighty" is translated in Genesis 10:9 in the Septuagint Greek OT (~3rd Century B.C.) as *gigas*, or "giant," indicating that at least some of the ancient peoples believed Nimrod was a giant. Other names proposed for Nimrod by various scholars are Baal of the Philistines and Phoenicians (Sidonians, Carthaginians, Tyrians, etc.), Marduk of the Babylonians, Gilgamesh and Ninurta of the Sumerians, or a deification of King Ninus of Nineveh by the Greeks. Deification of rulers was a common practice in OT times, so their arguments have merit with respect to proposing that Nimrod was deified.

So, what do the proponents of this view propose as the rationale for Nimrod having to do with the antichrist being racially black or dark skinned? Nimrod was the son of Cush, who was the son of Ham. Ham is considered by all theologians worth any salt as being the progenitor of all the African peoples. Cush is considered the father of some of the first inhabitants of both sides of the Red Sea, including the Arabian Peninsula, Sudan, and Ethiopia; the Cushite (or Kushite) Kingdom existed south of ancient Egypt in what is now Sudan. People from those regions are racially black or dark skinned. Furthermore, some argue that the leopard is identified more with Africa than Asia (but try telling that to folks in India who have a serious problem with leopards eating humans, pets, and livestock), which would then parallel and link the black spots of the leopard to the dark skin of the Ethiopian or the dark skin of Osiris, who is allegedly a deified Nimrod. Finally, connecting all the pieces, there are two dominant approaches that are taken by the antichrist-is-black theorists: (1) Nimrod is a pre-type of the final world ruler, and the final world ruler will have both his geographic origin like Nimrod's, meaning Babylon, i.e., modern Iraq, and his genetics like Nimrod's, meaning dark skinned or racially black; and (2) since Jeremiah 13:23 links the leopard to the Ethiopian of Africa, and since the beast of Revelation 13:2 is predominantly a leopard, then the antichrist must be like the Ethiopian, meaning black.

But, as I stated above, the leopard is also an Asian beast, meaning the antichrist could come from a place like Iraq, as will be discussed in Chapter 10. There are Iraqis of African descent, specifically descendants of slaves brought by Muslim slave traders, living in the Zubeir District of Basra, and they look like conventional sub-Saharan Africans. But even apart from Iraqis of African origin, if you look at the indigenous people of Iraq, olive to very dark skin is common there. Whether you want to take the African approach or the Asian approach, it's a safe bet that the antichrist will not have the pale skin tone of an American of western European extract such as myself. This as another argument against the antichrist being of European origin, thereby disqualifying the British monarchy.

Given that the world received Barack Obama with open arms and hailed him as a savior who would unite warring factions - laughable and pathetic in hindsight - because of his multi-racial, multi-cultural, multi-religious, and multi-national background, it's not a stretch to think that this pattern will be one of Satan's methodologies for securing adulation for his boy. Lest anyone think there are racist overtones to this supposition, consider that the wretched leaders of Europe like Hitler, Stalin, and the hedonistic royals of each country were white, and that the marauding warlords and dictators of Asia like the Khans, the Qins/Chins, Hirohito, and Mao Zedong were yellow. There is no room for assigning more wickedness to one race than another; all are wicked and, in any case, sin is a distinctly *human* race issue. As an aside, the Bible does not use the Hebrew or Greek words for race to uniquely assign skin color. I challenge anyone to prove that last statement wrong.

Chapter 8

JEWISH

Proponents of the antichrist-is-Muslim theory are very vocal about their opposition to the idea that the antichrist will be Jewish. One of their arguments is that the Bible nowhere states outright that the antichrist will be Jewish. This is a true statement, but then again, the Bible also nowhere states outright that he will be Muslim. Of course, Islam's origin from Mohammed post-dated the completion of the Biblical canon by five centuries, so it is logical that Islam would not be named by name. Still, if God had wanted to clue us into this coming religion and its messiah, or Mahdi, as major players in prophecy, He could have used prophetical terms like "the god of the crescent moon and star," or "out of the tents of Dedan and Sheba [Arabian peninsula] shall come a lawless one who will serve the god of the black stone," (the Black Stone is in the Kaaba in Mecca) but He did not. There are any number of ways God could have easily identified for us the coming

Muslim faith and a Muslim Mahdi using prophetical symbolism, but He did not. With respect to the antichrist-is-Muslim proponents' contention that there is no indication in the Bible that the antichrist will be Jewish, this is simply not true, for one only needs to understand key words in Scripture with some understanding of the original Biblical languages to unlock the answer, as we shall see below.

The antichrist-is-Muslim proponents make a second argument against the antichrist being Jewish. They say that Scripture does not support the following idea: the antichrist must be Jewish, because the Jews would not revere him if he weren't Jewish. The gist of their argument is that there is no Biblical evidence to indicate that the Jews will have any reverence toward or love for the antichrist. This argument is, also, simply not true.

Let us begin to unlock the issue.

[15] And the Lord said unto me, Take unto thee yet the instruments of a **foolish** shepherd. [16] For, lo, I will raise up a shepherd in the land, which shall not visit those that be cut off, neither shall seek the young one, nor heal that that is broken, nor feed that that standeth still: but he shall eat the flesh of the fat, and tear their claws in pieces. [17] Woe to the **idol** shepherd that leaveth the flock! the sword shall be upon his arm, and upon his right eye: his

arm shall be clean dried up, and his right eye shall be
utterly darkened.

Zechariah 11:15-17

We see in this passage a reference to a shepherd. Not only
a shepherd but a foolish and idol one. No, not idle, as in lazy,
but **idol**, as in one who is idolized - or worshipped. This is an
important concept, for whereas the Hebrew root word for idol,
elil, can be translated as "worthless" - and is translated as
"worthless" in a few instances in the KJV and other versions -
it is most often translated as "idol." The KJV translators
understood the context of the Zechariah passage above and got
it right. This certainly speaks against the argument that the
Jews won't worship this foolish shepherd; further evidence of
the adoration the Jews will initially have for the foolish
shepherd is presented in Chapter 10. But you may ask, even if
the Jews worship the foolish shepherd, how does being a
shepherd relate to the antichrist being Jewish?

Shepherds are important people in Scripture, both
practically in the daily life of Israel and prophetically in the
spiritual life of Israel. Recall that our Lord is called the Good
Shepherd. Granted, Scripture must have meaning both to the
people of Israel who first read and heard those words and to
later Gentiles who are saved through faith, but I would surmise
that the word "shepherd" would have far greater significance
to an Israelite than to a Gentile and would be interpreted by

said Israelite to be a Jew. Meditate on Micah 5:5, wherein "seven shepherds" will rise up to oppose the Assyrian (another name for the antichrist, as will be explained in Chapter 10), and you can see that a strong case can be made for interpreting the idol and foolish shepherd, i.e., the antichrist, as a Jew. It certainly has the ring of God's sense of parity and symbolism: the perfect number of seven good, Jewish shepherds against one foolish, Jewish shepherd. "In the land" of Zechariah 11:16 would indicate Israel to a Jew of the 6th Century B.C., further enforcing the idea that Zechariah speaks of a Jew. This foolish Jew will not fare well in a physical sense, because he will be severely wounded in his eye and arm, as attested to in Zechariah 11:17 and Revelation 13:3, wherein the antichrist receives an apparently mortal head wound. This is not an iron-clad argument proving the antichrist to be Jewish, but considering the evidence shown below, it's a nice start.

> [36] And the king shall do according to his will; and he shall exalt himself, and magnify himself above every god, and shall speak marvellous things against the God of gods, and shall prosper till the indignation be accomplished: for that that is determined shall be done. [37] Neither shall he regard the God of his fathers, nor the desire of women, nor regard any god: for he shall magnify himself above all. [38] But in his estate shall he honour the God of forces: and a god whom his fathers knew not shall he honour with gold, and silver, and with precious stones,

and pleasant things. [39] Thus shall he do in the most strong holds with a strange god, whom he shall acknowledge and increase with glory: and he shall cause them to rule over many, and shall divide the land for gain.

Daniel 11:36-39

Much speculation has been made about the meaning of "the God of his fathers" in Verse 37. Depending on which prophetical circle you run in, you may take that as meaning that God to be the Christian God, i.e., Jesus; or the Jewish God of Abraham, Isaac, and Jacob; or the Muslim god, i.e., Allah. The Christian God approach seems more common to Western Christians who see through European and American eyes, in reference to the belief by some students of prophecy that Charles, William, or some other European royal; or the Pope, Emmanuel Macron, Recep Erdogan, or Barack Obama will morph into the antichrist. The Jewish God approach resonates with unconverted but observant Jews and Messianic Jews (of course, the Messianic Jews are Christians who know that Jesus was and is that God), and the Muslim god approach resonates with Muslim converts to Christianity. On this last point, as stated previously, a significant movement has sprung up in the last decade or so from Christians of Islamic background that proposes that the antichrist will be a Muslim, one argument being that the Islamic Mahdi (messiah) is the polar opposite of Jesus and fits the description of the Biblical antichrist to a T.

To all this I say, using the argument stated above that OT Scripture must first have meaning to Jews before it has meaning to Gentiles, that in the very least the antichrist **must be Jewish**, for I doubt that any Jew reading Daniel 11:36-39 during Daniel's time and thereafter would think to ascribe "God of his fathers" to anyone other than the God of Abraham, Isaac, and Jacob. To those observant Jews living at the time of the antichrist's ascension, it will have great meaning to them for one of their own who they thought was their long-awaited Messiah to suddenly exalt himself above everyone and everything, then forbid the daily sacrifices and install an idol of himself in the temple. They will likely make the connection that this guy is the guy who is not honoring the God of their fathers.

As for the Christian God, well, I suppose that it's within the realm of possibility in the sense that Jesus was and is the God of the Jews' fathers. After all, it was He who walked in the Garden of Eden in the cool of the day, seeking the two who were suddenly lost; it was He who appeared to Abraham to tell of the coming birth of Isaac; He who saved the terrified Hagar from certain death in the desert; He who wrestled with Jacob; He who went up in the flames of offering before Samson's parents; He who appeared to Moses in the burning bush; He who was the fire by night and the cloud by day; He who stood above the Mercy Seat; He who revealed His back in full glory to Moses; and He who met the children of Israel in the wilderness at the foot of Mount Horeb.

Regarding the Muslim god, some make an argument that the term "God of his fathers" refers to all the gods that the people of the Arabian peninsula worshipped before Mohammed declared Allah to be the one and only god. They argue that the Hebrew word for God in the passage, *elohe*, is a masculine **plural** construct noun, meaning that it could be translated as "gods," as in "gods of his fathers." The Muslim god proponents thus argue that this is one of several points to indicate that the antichrist must be Muslim, because: (1) before the monotheistic Islam came into being in Arabia, the people of Arabia worshipped many different gods, and (2) the God of the Jews and the Christians is singular, such that Jews' and Christians' "fathers" never worshipped "gods":

4 Hear, O Israel: The Lord our God is one Lord.

Deuteronomy 6:4

30 I and my Father are one.

John 10:30

Hmm, what to make of this? The plural Hebrew form for God is used often in the OT and is translated routinely as singular God, so their argument is not a great one, particularly in consideration that the first verse of the Bible uses one plural form for the name of God, *Elohim*.

67

¹ In the beginning God [Elohim] created the heaven and the earth.

Genesis 1:1

We see the first indication of God as the Trinity yet one God in the very first verse of the Bible, so there should be no issue of translating it in the singular form in Daniel 11:37.

Perhaps the Lord left "God of his fathers" purposely ambiguous to allow for all three gods to be understood, depending on the angle from which it is being viewed. For those of you in the crowd screaming, "There can only be one meaning in a passage, not multiple!! That's not good hermeneutics for conducting good exegesis!", I would suggest that it doesn't matter from which angle one is viewing the passage; it still means that this beast will not regard the god or gods of his predecessors, and that **is** the one meaning. Maybe it could mean he rejects the Christian God, maybe the Muslim god, but I feel more certain that the meaning of Daniel 11:37 is that he will first reject the God of his Jewish fathers.

Adding more ammunition to my argument, I provide the following:

⁴³ I am come in my Father's name, and ye receive me not: if **another** [*allos*, i.e., another of the same kind as opposed

68

to *heteros*, another of a different kind] shall come in his own name, him ye will receive.

John 5:43

Greek often can be more precise than English, for where we might use one word that can have multiple meanings requiring context to decipher the intended meaning, Greek can remove the burden of context to tell us precisely what is intended. Jesus is prophesying of a time in the future when **another** (*allos*) of Jesus's kind, meaning a Jew, will be welcomed by the Jews; another of a totally different kind, meaning a Gentile, is not in view here, for had a Gentile been intended, then *heteros* would have been used.

Irrespective of interpretation of Scripture, a strong argument from logic can be made that the guy **must** be Jewish, for how could the Jews ever accept a *goy*, a defiled and unclean man of the nations (*goyim*)? He will be an impostor, a poser, a deceiver, one who uses something familiar and seemingly true to hoodwink humanity. This is Satan's oldest trick in the Book.

⁴ And the serpent said unto the woman, Ye shall not surely die.

Genesis 3:4

Chapter 9

TRIBE OF DAN

The Tribe of Dan is an interesting group of folks, a truly motley crew. This tribe serves as the basis of the theory of British Israelism, the belief that much of Europe and even America descended from the ten Lost Tribes of Israel. I was going to prepare a detailed breakdown on how this theory came about, but then I found that *Wikipedia* has a nice summation of it at https://en.wikipedia.org/wiki/British_Israelism. In short, the *Wikipedia* article links the ancient, nomadic Scythians of eastern Europe and Asia to the Sacae, or Isaac-ites, to the Saxons (Sac's sons – Isaac's sons), to invaders of England from Denmark (the land of the Tribe of Dan). Here it is:

> Herodotus [ancient Greek historian] reported that the ancient Persians called all the Scythians *Sacae*, but that they called themselves *Scoloti*. However, a modern comparison among the forms given in other ancient languages suggests *Skuda* was their name. Ancient

writers, such as Josephus and Jerome would associate the Scythians with the peoples of Gog and Magog, but British Israelist etymologists would see in *Sacae* a name derived from the biblical "Isaac", claiming that the appearance of the Scythians where they claimed the Lost Tribes were last documented also supported a connection. Further, British Israelists find support in the superficial resemblance between King Jehu's pointed headdress [on the Black Obelisk of Assyrian King Shalmaneser III in the British Museum] and that of the captive Saka king seen to the far right on the Behistun Rock [a multilingual inscription and large rock relief on a cliff at Mount Behistun in the Kermanshah Province in western Iran]. The chain of etymological identification leading from Isaac to the *Sacae* was continued to the Saxons (interpreted as Sac's sons - the sons of Isaac), who are portrayed as invading England from Denmark, the 'land of the Tribe of Dan'. They saw the same tribal name, left by the wanderers, in the Dar*dan*elles, the *Dan*ube, Mace*don*ia, *Dun*kirk, *Dun*glow in Ireland, *Dun*dee in Scotland, and Lon*don*, and ascribed to this lost tribe the mythical Irish *Tuatha Dé Danann*.

Some adherents further claim that the British Royal Family is directly descended from the line of King David. Citing the *Book of Jeremiah*, they claim that the daughters of Zedekiah [one in particular, Tea Tephi] fled to Egypt, then 'the isles' in the sea, which they interpret as Ireland. The descendants of these princesses are said to have crossed to England where they became ancestors of the monarchs. The Stone of Scone, used in coronations of Scottish, English and British monarchs for centuries, is claimed to be none other than the pillow stone used by biblical patriarch, Jacob.

I will add to this that the British Israelism proponents claim that the words Britain and British are derived from the Hebrew *b'rith*, which means *covenant*. Thus, in their minds the British are just as much the children of the covenant as those who actually call themselves that moniker, specifically the Jewish organization B'nai B'rith (Children of the Covenant).

Perhaps a few Danites did escape the Assyrians when they conquered the ten Northern Tribes of Israel in 722 B.C. and took their madness, murder, and mayhem on the road throughout Europe, but modern scholars agree that the British Israelism theory is without weighty, empirical support. The fact that cults like the Worldwide Church of God and its cultish founder, Herbert Armstrong, supported it should be cause for pause to any student of prophecy for considering it a legitimate theory. Nevertheless, it does make the point that Dan has earned quite the reputation for himself as a ne'er-do-well.

However, it's not like the Tribe of Dan didn't have a few stellar moments in their history, such as the judge Samson giving the Philistines a beat-down on a fairly routine basis, but even then, Samson had some serious character flaws, like fraternizing with pagans and failing to control his sexual passions. Samson is an excellent example to demonstrate that God specializes in making straight licks with crooked sticks. Yet, there is at least one crooked stick from Dan that is just too crooked for God to want to do anything positive with; this is the case for the antichrist.

Early in his history, Dan was identified by his father, Israel, as a trouble maker.

[16] Dan shall judge his people, as one of the tribes of Israel. [17] Dan shall be a serpent [Hebrew *nakash*, a fiery, bronze serpent] by the way, an adder [Hebrew *shephiphon*; Greek *cerastes*, i.e., the 2-horned Arabian horned viper, a snake that lies beneath the sand until its prey wanders into its path] in the path, that biteth the horse heels, so that his rider shall fall backward. [18] I have waited for thy salvation, O Lord.

Genesis 49:16-18

Arabian horned viper

So, Israel calls Dan a 2-horned, fiery, bronze serpent, reminiscent of that same kind of deceptive creature that infested the Garden of Eden. This creature is an ambush predator, lying in wait to catch its prey unaware. Sounds very satanic and beastly.

After Israel's proclamation that Dan will be a trouble maker, he says something in Verse 18 that seems completely out of context, as if he's gone into a trance of sorts and sees a vision of the future Messiah who will oppose Dan. The commentaries are all over the page for what Israel meant by this seemingly out-of-context statement about "salvation," but some make the connection to the coming Messiah in opposition to the antichrist. Quoting from the famous 19th Century commentary by German Lutheran theologians, Keil and Delitzsch:

> But whilst the Targumists and several [early Church] fathers connect the serpent in the way with Samson, by many others the serpent in the way is supposed to be Antichrist.

Thus, by making a connection to the antichrist, Israel's proclamation of waiting "for thy salvation," i.e., Jesus, makes sense and bolsters the idea that out of the Tribe of Dan will come the antichrist.

More about Dan must be considered. In the following passages, we see that the children of Dan were the first recorded among the 12 Tribes to openly curse God; the first tribe to lead the nation of Israel into idolatry; and the first tribe to be selected by King Jeroboam for setting up graven images after King Solomon died. There seems to be a proclivity among this tribe for blasphemy, idolatry, and violence.

> [11] And the Israelitish woman's son blasphemed the name of the Lord, and cursed. And they brought him unto Moses: (and his mother's name was Shelomith, the daughter of Dibri, of the tribe of Dan).

> Leviticus 24:11

Since the verse above presents the blasphemer's link to Israel as through the mother, I want to sidetrack a bit here to discuss the issue of matriarchy versus patriarchy and how it affects the constitution of the antichrist. I once had an interesting conversation with an Israeli cigar shop owner whose shop in Jerusalem's Ben Yehuda Square had been severely damaged in December 2001 by a Hamas suicide bomber that killed several teenagers outside his shop. This shop owner used Leviticus 24:11 as his proof text to explain why modern Jews view Jewish lineage as through the mother rather than through the father, in direct contrast with how the majority of Scripture views it. He said, "Everyone knows who their mother is but not necessarily who their father is." His words, not mine.

In contrast to modern Jews, the Muslims identify lineage through the father – if the dad is a Muslim, the children must follow suit. I have done internet searches and found the children of unions of Muslim men with Jewish women, so people of both Jewish and Muslim heritage do exist. Remember this dynamic for my previous point about the antichrist being multi-everything.

Now, returning to our main topic, Dan is quite the beast. Israel said he would be a snake, but Moses saw something else that was beastly about Dan.

²² And of Dan he said, Dan is a lion's whelp [offspring]: he shall leap from Bashan.

Deuteronomy 33:22

Some scholars suggest that this is a picture of Dan's movement from Bashan in northeastern Israel, where the Ammonites had pushed them out of the plains and into the mountains, to northwestern Israel where the Sidonians existed. The association with a lion is seen by some as referring to Dan's violent nature. Joshua and Judges record this.

⁴⁷ And the coast of the children of Dan went out too little for them: therefore the children of Dan went up to fight against Leshem, [This is also known as Laish in Judges 18, another version of Dan's attack on the city. Laish translates as *lion.*] and took it, and smote it with the edge

of the sword, and possessed it, and dwelt therein, and called Leshem, Dan, after the name of Dan their father.

Joshua 19:47

⁷ And they took the things which Micah had made, and the priest which he had, and came unto Laish, unto a people that were at quiet and secure: and they smote them with the edge of the sword, and burnt the city with fire. ²⁸ And there was no deliverer, because it was far from Zidon, and they had no business with any man; and it was in the valley that lieth by Bethrehob. And they built a city, and dwelt therein. ²⁹ And they called the name of the city Dan, after the name of Dan their father, who was born unto Israel: howbeit the name of the city was Laish at the first. ³⁰ And the children of Dan set up the graven image: and Jonathan, the son of Gershom, the son of Manasseh, he and his sons were priests to the tribe of Dan until the day of the captivity of the land. ³¹ And they set them up Micah's graven image, which he made, all the time that the house of God was in Shiloh.

Judges 18:7,28-31

In addition to Dan's violent nature, the above Judges 18 passage also describes Dan's propensity for idolatry, and it is further recorded for us in 1 Kings 12.

²⁶ And Jeroboam said in his heart, Now shall the kingdom return to the house of David: ²⁷ If this people go

up to do sacrifice in the house of the Lord at Jerusalem, then shall the heart of this people turn again unto their lord, even unto Rehoboam king of Judah, and they shall kill me, and go again to Rehoboam king of Judah. [28] Whereupon the king took counsel, and made two calves of gold, and said unto them, It is too much for you to go up to Jerusalem: behold thy gods, O Israel, which brought thee up out of the land of Egypt. [29] And he set the one in Bethel, and the other put he in Dan. [30] And this thing became a sin: for the people went to worship before the one, even unto Dan.

1 Kings 12:26-30

Another powerful piece of evidence to suggest that the antichrist will be from the Tribe of Dan is the following.

[1] And after these things I saw four angels standing on the four corners of the earth, holding the four winds of the earth, that the wind should not blow on the earth, nor on the sea, nor on any tree. [2] And I saw another angel ascending from the east, having the seal of the living God: and he cried with a loud voice to the four angels, to whom it was given to hurt the earth and the sea, [3] Saying, Hurt not the earth, neither the sea, nor the trees, till we have sealed the servants of our God in their foreheads. [4] And I heard the number of them which were sealed: and there were sealed an hundred and forty and

four thousand of all the tribes of the children of Israel. [5] Of the tribe of Juda were sealed twelve thousand. Of the tribe of Reuben were sealed twelve thousand. Of the tribe of Gad were sealed twelve thousand. [6] Of the tribe of Aser were sealed twelve thousand. Of the tribe of Nephthalim were sealed twelve thousand. Of the tribe of Manasses [eldest son of Joseph] were sealed twelve thousand. [7] Of the tribe of Simeon were sealed twelve thousand. Of the tribe of Levi were sealed twelve thousand. Of the tribe of Issachar were sealed twelve thousand.[8] Of the tribe of Zabulon were sealed twelve thousand. Of the tribe of Joseph [i.e., Ephraim, youngest son of Joseph and the largest tribe of the ten Northern Tribes] were sealed twelve thousand. Of the tribe of Benjamin were sealed twelve thousand.

Revelation 7:1-8

You may be wondering why I present this as evidence for the antichrist's lineage as potentially being from Dan, since Dan is not mentioned in this passage. **And that's the point.** Dan does not get to participate in this end-times, mass, evangelistic outreach. It appears to me that God is really irritated with this tribe, and one member of it in particular.

One final point must be made about Dan, and it relates to the phrase "lion's whelp" in Deuteronomy 33:32. Dan is not the only son of the patriarch Israel who was referred to as a "lion's whelp."

> [9] Judah is a lion's whelp [offspring]: from the prey, my son, thou art gone up: he stooped down, he couched as a lion, and as an old lion; who shall rouse him up?
>
> Genesis 49:9

Hmmm, very strange. Israel went on to say in Genesis 49:10 that the "sceptre shall not depart from Judah, nor a lawgiver from between his feet, until Shiloh [Jesus] come; and unto him shall the gathering of the people be," referring to the Tribe of Judah being the royal tribe from which Jesus came. Jesus is the Lion of the Tribe of Judah (Revelation 5:5) and has the attributes of His Father, for Jesus told his disciples in John 14:9 that "he that hath seen me hath seen the Father," and in John 5:19 that the "Son can do nothing of himself, but what he seeth the Father do: for what things soever he doeth, these also doeth the Son likewise." Like Father, like Son. Thus, the Father is also a lion of sorts. But Their chief antagonist through all of human history also is referred to as a lion.

> [8] Be sober, be vigilant; because your adversary the devil, as a roaring lion, walketh about, seeking whom he may devour:
>
> 1 Peter 5:8

Two fathers, two sons. Two lions, two lions' sons. The One lion's Son seeks to empower people; the other lion's son seeks to devour people. Shades of the war between the Seed of the woman and the seed of the serpent:

> ¹⁵ And I will put enmity between thee and the woman, and between thy seed and her seed; it shall bruise thy head, and thou shalt bruise his heel.

Genesis 3:15

Therefore, I rest my case for the antichrist being a Danite.

Chapter 10

IRAQI

Part 1 – Introduction

I raq. Who in their right mind would ascribe any significance to Iraq, a backwater, developing nation constantly embroiled in controversies within and without? If Iraqis are not literally or politically fighting the Iranians, they're fighting the Saudis; if they're not fighting the Saudis, they're fighting the Kuwaitis; if they're not fighting the Kuwaitis, they're fighting within against the Kurds; if they're not fighting within against the Kurds, they're fighting within against ISIS. Then there are skirmishes with the Turks and Israelis, and finally, add in a couple of wars with the US, which is now Iraq's major benefactor. But it will not always be this way because, according to Daniel 7, the US (the wings of the lion-with-eagle's-wings beast) will eventually be removed as a major benefactor to Iraq. In a scenario where a leading oil producer and refiner like the US is humbled and the dollar is deflated into oblivion, it may pave the way for the Saudis and Iraqis to team up as a buffer against their mutual enemy, Iran; Iraq, like the Saudis, has massive oil reserves. Combine these possibilities with the fact that money is being pumped in by the United Nations (UN) and contributing countries to make the ancient city of Babylon into a center of culture and tourism. Recall that Saddam Hussein did major reconstruction in Babylon in his fanciful attempts to liken himself to Nebuchadnezzar, the greatest king of Babylon. There are even rumors that the US, Russia, European Union, and UN have drafted a resolution to move the UN headquarters from New York to a rebuilt Babylon to gain new space for physical expansion and to avoid the political and legal constraints of being in the US. Or perhaps a US president and a political party will get some backbones and tire of funding an organization that routinely votes against US and Israel, thereby defunding the UN, compelling it to move to that symbolic base of ancient, anti-God world government. Whatever the means, Scripture has ample information to indicate that Iraq will be a major player in future, world events.

I must warn the reader that this chapter is long, but its length is of necessity, and it is for this reason that I have broken it up into four parts. One reviewer of the draft of this book commented that I spent a disproportionate portion of the book on this topic, which seemed to him lopsided relative to the other chapters. But this topic must be fully examined, for the dominant theories have become so ingrained in their proponents' and adherents' minds that it will take the equivalent of a textual sledge hammer to dislodge them. No doubt there are other theories, but the dominant theories are that the antichrist will be Turkish, Syrian, American, or European, in particular Roman. All these theories have serious flaws and are, in my thinking, just flat wrong. The importance of this issue cannot be overstated, because we need to look at the correct location of the antichrist's origin to optimize our chances of identifying him before his rise to power. Therefore, I encourage readers to hang in there and work through to the end.

Before we dive into this chapter, we first need to decide if we believe that prophecies can be fulfilled twice or only once. This is a critical issue, because the ramifications of that belief, whatever belief it may be, are significant with respect to searching for clues in the prophetical record regarding who the antichrist is. If we say prophecies can be fulfilled only once but, in reality, they can be fulfilled twice, then we will miss information that helps us unlock who he is and what his destiny will be. Conversely, if we say prophecies can be fulfilled twice but, in reality, they can be fulfilled only once, then we may go down rabbit holes leading to wrong conclusions. Either way, if we are wrong in our selection, we miss the truth, and missing the truth leads to costly, wrong decision making, much like the man who thinks his engine needs a costly repair when it only needs cheap, new spark plugs.

The issue of single or double fulfillment of prophecy has been a heated debate within the theological community, but this is not the venue for delving deeply into that debate. For anyone who cares to investigate the debate further, a good starting point is David Jeremiah's excellent paper, *The Principle of Double Fulfillment in Interpreting Prophecy*, which can be found at https://biblicalstudies.org.uk/pdf/grace-journal/13-2_13.pdf.

Rather than keep the reading audience on pins and needles regarding my own position on the matter, I will simply state that I believe prophecies can be fulfilled twice, or rather that prophecies can be partially fulfilled by events of the past and then entirely fulfilled by events of the future. A simplified way of explaining double fulfillment is that two events separated by time can have enough points of agreement that one prophecy can describe both events; however, the prophecy typically has a few details that were not fulfilled by the first event and can be fulfilled only by the second event, as if the first fulfillment is a subset of the second and final fulfillment. As an example, prophecies in Isaiah and Jeremiah of God's judgment on the king of Babylon and on Babylon itself would look to a Jew of the centuries following Babylon's conquest by the Medo-Persian alliance as if those prophecies had been fulfilled. Yet, upon closer inspection, not every point of those prophecies was fulfilled and indicate a future fulfillment when all points of the prophecy will be fulfilled.

Before moving on, we need to discuss another approach to interpreting prophecy that is abhorrent, dangerous, and to be avoided at all cost: preterism. I feel compelled to warn readers of its dangers. The preterists, or those who insist that virtually all the prophecies of the Bible have been fulfilled, even Revelation, reject the notion that there are prophecies yet to be fulfilled. For instance, preterists see prophecies out of Isaiah and Jeremiah about the destruction of Babylon as nothing more than predictions of the destruction of Babylon by the Medes and Persians that have been fulfilled, with no potentiality for a future, final fulfillment. Their approach is based on allegory and removes the Biblical text from its plain meaning and assumes that, when the preterist doesn't think the plain text makes sense, there is some deeper, spiritual meaning. They basically dismiss the entire book of Revelation as allegory and spiritualize it, saying that it was fulfilled with the destruction of Jerusalem in 70 A.D., and nullify the physical return of Jesus to the earth. Perversely false and heretical. It leaves interpretation of Scripture up to the imagination of the preterist and disconnects it from the meaning God intended. The Biblical text often uses symbolism to describe events, but symbolism can be unlocked by using Scripture to unlock Scripture and need not be allegorized to guess at some spiritualized meaning. A true danger of their heresy is that it nullifies prophecies of warning to prepare for the coming difficulties, such that the Body of Christ possesses a host of deer-in-the-headlights Christians who have no idea what to make of the events recited in Matthew 24, many of which are occurring now and clearly indicate the soon return of Jesus.

Part 2 – The Prophecies

Now, let's dive into the prophecies. This first prophecy is from Isaiah 10 and describes the "Assyrian," whom God uses to chastise Israel because of its unrighteousness and hypocrisy, but then God punishes him because of his own boastfulness and failure to recognize that he is but a tool in God's hand. The importance of the "Assyrian" for this chapter is that ancient Assyria, including its capital city, Nineveh, falls largely within the boundaries of modern Iraq. At first glance, it appears as if the prophecy was only for a near-future fulfillment from the time of Isaiah when the ten Northern Tribes of Israel were conquered by the Assyrians, the process of which was completed in 722 B.C. when Sargon II overran Samaria in northern Israel. But there are clues that indicate its ultimate fulfillment will be when the antichrist conquers modern Israel. We'll discuss the clues after the prophecy.

> [1] Woe unto them that decree unrighteous decrees, and that write grievousness which they have prescribed; [2] To turn aside the needy from judgment, and to take away the right from the poor of my people, that widows may

be their prey, and that they may rob the fatherless! ³ And what will ye do in the day of visitation, and in the desolation which shall come from far? to whom will ye flee for help? and where will ye leave your glory? ⁴ Without me they shall bow down under the prisoners, and they shall fall under the slain. For all this his anger is not turned away, but his hand is stretched out still. ⁵ O Assyrian [antichrist], the rod of mine anger, and the staff in their hand is mine indignation. ⁶ I will send him against an hypocritical nation [Israel], and against the people of my wrath will I give him a charge, to take the spoil, and to take the prey, and to tread them down like the mire of the streets. ⁷ Howbeit he meaneth not so, neither doth his heart think so; but it is in his heart to destroy and cut off nations not a few. ⁸ For he saith, Are not my princes altogether kings? ⁹ Is not Calno as Carchemish [both are in Syria]? is not Hamath as Arpad [both are in Syria]? is not Samaria [the current Palestinian Territory] as Damascus [in Syria]? ¹⁰ As my hand hath found the kingdoms of the idols, and whose graven images did excel them of Jerusalem and of Samaria; ¹¹ Shall I not, as I have done unto Samaria and her idols, so do to Jerusalem and her idols? ¹² Wherefore it shall come to pass, that when the Lord hath performed his whole work upon mount Zion and on Jerusalem, I will punish the fruit of the stout heart of the king of

Assyria, and the glory of his high looks. [13] For he saith, By the strength of my hand I have done it, and by my wisdom; for I am prudent: and I have removed the bounds of the people, and have robbed their treasures, and I have put down the inhabitants like a valiant man: [14] And my hand hath found as a nest the riches of the people: and as one gathereth eggs that are left, have I gathered all the earth; and there was none that moved the wing, or opened the mouth, or peeped. [15] Shall the axe boast itself against him that heweth therewith? or shall the saw magnify itself against him that shaketh it? as if the rod should shake itself against them that lift it up, or as if the staff should lift up itself, as if it were no wood. [16] Therefore shall the Lord, the Lord of hosts, send among his fat ones leanness; and under his glory he shall kindle a burning like the burning of a fire. [17] And the light of Israel shall be for a fire, and his Holy One for a flame: and it shall burn and devour his thorns and his briers in one day; [18] And shall consume the glory of his forest, and of his fruitful field, both soul and body: and they shall be as when a standard-bearer fainteth. [19] And the rest of the trees of his forest shall be few, that a child may write them. [20] And it shall come to pass in that day, that the remnant of Israel, and such as are escaped of the house of Jacob, shall no more again **stay upon** [love, revere, follow] him [antichrist] that smote them; but shall stay upon the Lord, the Holy One of Israel, in truth. [21] The remnant shall return, even the remnant of Jacob, unto the mighty God. [22] For though thy people Israel be as the sand of the sea, yet a remnant of them shall return: the consumption decreed shall overflow with righteousness. [23] For the Lord God of hosts shall make a consumption, even determined, in the midst of all the land. [24] Therefore thus saith the Lord God of hosts, O my people that dwellest in Zion, be not afraid of the Assyrian: he shall smite thee with a rod, and shall lift up his staff against thee, after the manner of Egypt. [25] For yet a very little while, and the indignation shall cease, and mine anger in their destruction. [26] And the Lord of hosts shall stir up a scourge for him according to the slaughter of Midian at the rock of Oreb: and as his rod was upon the sea, so shall he lift it up after the manner of Egypt. [27] And it shall come to pass in that day, that his burden shall be taken away from off thy shoulder, and his yoke from off thy neck, and the yoke shall be destroyed because of the anointing.

Isaiah 10:1-27

We see terms like:

1. "desolation" in Verse 3, reminiscent of Daniel 9:27; 11:31; and 12:11 that discuss the "abomination that maketh desolate," which is when the antichrist enters the temple

and sets up an image of himself, "shewing himself that he is God" (2 Thessalonians 2:4);

2. "in one day" in Verse 17, referring to "that day" of Verses 20 and 27, all of which refer to the "day of the Lord" found in over 40 verses of the Bible and which refers to the day of the Lord's retribution on the wicked at Armageddon;

3. "indignation" in Verse 25, bringing to mind the "indignation," or attack on Israel, of Isaiah 26:20, against which God will protect Israel when He punishes the "inhabitants of the earth" (Isaiah 26:21). An attack on Israel as a global event in which many nations and people groups participate has yet to happen;

4. In Verse 20, "the remnant of Israel... shall no more again stay upon [be dedicated to, affectionate toward] him [the Assyrian/Iraqi antichrist] that smote them; but shall stay upon the Lord, the Holy One of Israel, in truth." The Israelites never had any fondness for Sargon II or any Assyrian king, but they will have affection for their false messiah and will make a covenant with him – "he shall confirm the covenant with many for one week" (Daniel 9:27), i.e., the "covenant of death" from Isaiah 28:15,18 - which is the covenant with the antichrist that God will nullify and replace with affection toward Him;

5. Finally, "his burden shall be taken away from off thy shoulder" in Verse 27, which speaks of a time in the future

when Israel will be free of this Assyrian. Israel was never freed by the Assyrians after the conquest of 722 B.C., because the ten Northern Tribes were resettled and dispersed by the Assyrians, so this is a point of difference from history that indicates something yet to come.

The phrase "stay upon him that smote them" in Point 4 above is an obvious blow to the antichrist-is-Muslim cadre's argument that the Bible doesn't state that the Jews will revere him or otherwise highly regard him. In any case, the Isaiah 10 passage means that this prophecy speaks of a future fulfillment by an Assyrian, the antichrist, of Iraqi origin.

Next in line for discussion is a prophecy from Isaiah 14 that is famous for its supposed naming of the devil, i.e., it allegedly provides his real name. The following Isaiah 14 passage is a tough passage to properly interpret. Even the non-preterist, single-fulfillment folks who believe there is yet still much prophecy to be fulfilled, especially Revelation, see this passage as having been fulfilled entirely in the past by the aforesaid Medes and Persians. For those in the audience unfamiliar with Babylonian history, the Medo-Persian confederacy conquered Babylon in the 6th Century B.C. when they dammed up and diverted the Euphrates River and walked into Babylon under the city gates that previously had extended downward into the river. Let's examine the passage and then parse it afterwards.

¹ For the Lord will have mercy on Jacob, and will yet choose Israel, and set them in their own land: and the strangers shall be joined with them, and they shall cleave to the house of Jacob. ² And the people shall take them, and bring them to their place: and the house of Israel shall possess them in the land of the Lord for servants and handmaids: and they shall take them captives, whose captives they were; and they shall rule over their oppressors. ³ And it shall come to pass in the day that the Lord shall give thee rest from thy sorrow, and from thy fear, and from the hard bondage wherein thou wast made to serve, ⁴ That thou shalt take up this proverb against the king of Babylon, and say, How hath the oppressor ceased! the golden city ceased! ⁵ The Lord hath broken the staff of the wicked, and the sceptre of the rulers. ⁶ He who smote the people in wrath with a continual stroke, he that ruled the nations in anger, is persecuted, and none hindereth. ⁷ The whole earth is at rest, and is quiet: they break forth into singing. ⁸ Yea, the fir trees rejoice at thee, and the cedars of Lebanon, saying, Since thou art laid down, no feller is come up against us. ⁹ Hell from beneath is moved for thee to meet thee at thy coming: it stirreth up the dead for thee, even all the chief ones of the earth; it hath raised up from their thrones all the kings of the nations. ¹⁰ All they shall speak and say unto thee, Art thou also become weak as we? art

thou become like unto us? [11] Thy pomp is brought down to the grave, and the noise of thy viols: the worm is spread under thee, and the worms cover thee. [12] How art thou fallen from heaven, O Lucifer [shining one], son of the morning! how art thou cut down to the ground, which didst weaken the nations! [13] For thou hast said in thine heart, I will ascend into heaven, I will exalt my throne above the stars of God: I will sit also upon the mount of the congregation, in the sides of the north: [14] I will ascend above the heights of the clouds; I will be like the most High. [15] Yet thou shalt be brought down to hell, to the sides of the pit. [16] They that see thee shall narrowly look upon thee, and consider thee, saying, Is this the man that made the earth to tremble, that did shake kingdoms; [17] That made the world as a wilderness, and destroyed the cities thereof; that opened not the house of his prisoners? [18] All the kings of the nations, even all of them, lie in glory, every one in his own house. [19] But thou art cast out of thy grave like an abominable branch, and as the raiment of those that are slain, thrust through with a sword, that go down to the stones of the pit; as a carcass trodden under feet. [20] Thou shalt not be joined with them in burial, because thou hast destroyed thy land, and slain thy people: the seed of evildoers shall never be renowned. [21] Prepare slaughter for his children for the iniquity of their fathers; that they do not rise, nor possess the land, nor fill the face of the world with cities. ²² For I will rise up against them, saith the Lord of hosts, and cut off from Babylon the name, and remnant, and son, and nephew, saith the Lord. ²³ I will also make it a possession for the bittern, and pools of water: and I will sweep it with the besom of destruction, saith the Lord of hosts. ²⁴ The Lord of hosts hath sworn, saying, Surely as I have thought, so shall it come to pass; and as I have purposed, so shall it stand: ²⁵ That I will break the Assyrian in my land, and upon my mountains tread him under foot: then shall his yoke depart from off them, and his burden depart from off their shoulders. ²⁶ This is the purpose that is purposed upon the whole earth: and this is the hand that is stretched out upon all the nations. ²⁷ For the Lord of hosts hath purposed, and who shall disannul it? and his hand is stretched out, and who shall turn it back? ²⁸ In the year that king Ahaz died was this burden. [A "burden" is Biblical terminology for "prophecy"; do not construe it to mean that Isaiah 14 only applied to the time of Ahaz] ²⁹ Rejoice not thou, whole Palestina, because the rod of him that smote thee is broken: for out of the serpent's [Satan's] root shall come forth a cockatrice [antichrist], and his fruit shall be a fiery flying serpent [saraph]. ³⁰ And the firstborn of the poor shall feed, and the needy shall lie down in safety: and I will kill thy root with famine, and he shall slay thy remnant. ³¹ Howl, O gate; cry, O city; thou, whole Palestina, art dissolved: for there shall come from the north a smoke, and none shall be alone in his appointed times. [32] What shall one then answer the messengers of the nation? That the Lord hath founded Zion, and the poor of his people shall trust in it.

Isaiah 14

There are clues in Isaiah 14 that indicate both the preterist and non-preterist, single-fulfillment approaches are incorrect, for there are prophecies in it about the Jews that have yet to be fulfilled. Plainly stated, Isaiah 14's focus is on the antichrist, the most powerful, evil, and final king of Babylon. Though there are many kings that incurred the wrath of God in times past, none have stirred up His sense of repulsion, revulsion, and rage as has this last king of Babylon. He is also called the "Assyrian." Babylon and Assyria, ancient enemies, are both in Iraq, and this king is both Babylonian and Assyrian by birth, something that cannot be said of any ancient king.

We must be careful to not assign this passage to Satan or to any angelic being. Many people do make this connection because of the mention of Lucifer in Verse 12 in some Bible versions (but not all), which commentators commonly and mistakenly equate to Satan. Lucifer, which is the Latin word that translates from the Hebrew *helel*, or "shining one," was transliterated from the Latin translation of the Hebrew text by the KJV, New KJV, and Wycliffe translators as a proper name. But we must follow the clues that suggest otherwise:

1. The dead kings of the earth consider him their comrade, as one of them, in Verses 9 and 10;

2. He is covered with worms as a dead carcass in Verses 11 and 19, respectively;

3. He is called a man in Verse 16;

4. He destroys his own land and his own people in Verse 20, another indicator that he will be a Jew;

5. He is called the Assyrian in Verse 25.

The man is entirely delusional and has the most over-inflated view of himself of any human in history. These are not terms used for a fallen angel such as Ole Slewfoot; if you want to see a description of that rapscallion, turn your attention to Ezekiel 28:11-19. Satan is a *nakash*, the Hebrew word used in Genesis 3:14-15 to describe a fiery, bronze serpent.

> [14] And the Lord God said unto the serpent [nakash], Because thou hast done this, thou art cursed above all cattle, and above every beast of the field; upon thy belly shalt thou go, and dust shalt thou eat all the days of thy life:
>
> Genesis 3:14

Time and space do not permit me to explain all the points from Scripture to show that Satan is a fiery, bronze serpent in appearance, or at least has the ability to appear as such (yes, OK, 2 Corinthians 11:14 says he also can present himself as an angel of light), but suffice it to say that Satan is not a man and should not be equated to one.

Turning our attention to the Jews, the promises made to them in Verses 1 to 3 of Isaiah 14 have patently **not** been fulfilled. These verses did not apply to the Jews when they returned from Babylonian captivity to Israel during the ministry of Nehemiah, for he was opposed by Sanballat and his associates, and no people group in its entirety after the time of Isaiah has **ever** served the collective nation of Israel or suffered the fate of being their captives. The Maccabees from Judas Maccabee and after in the 2nd and 1st Centuries B.C. do not qualify either, for their reign was filled with turmoil and eventually ended with the ascension of that profane vassal to Rome, Herod the Great. No, Isaiah 14:1-3 parallel Daniel 12, Ezekiel 40-48, Romans 11, Revelation 7 and 14, and a host of other passages that proclaim the children of Israel will be reestablished in the land and experience peace and prosperity when Jesus rules on earth after His Second Coming. This is an end-times prophecy about an end-times Babylonian/ Assyrian/Iraqi antichrist who will be destroyed, resulting in Israel's restoration unto God. Let me be clear about this: I am firing a shot across the bow of those who teach that wicked doctrine of replacement theology, which teaches that God has forever cast off the Jews and passed on their blessings to the Gentile Church.

But there is more in Isaiah about the Assyrian. Isaiah 30 and 31 both speak of a time when Israel will be restored and Mount Zion will be exalted among the people, because God will fight for it and remove all sorrow from them. Jews in Jerusalem exalt Mount Zion now - or at least what they believe is Mount Zion, since there is new evidence to indicate it is located in the old City of David rather than under the Temple Mount complex - but not without sorrow, for they have a Wailing Wall, and the land of Israel does not possess the glory that is ascribed to it in these passages. Within the context of these passages is the "Assyrian" who will be defeated, indicating a future restoration after a future foe from Iraq is vanquished by the Lord.

Let us now examine the Isaiah 30 and 31 passages. Both refer to the future defeat of a coming Assyrian (Iraqi).

[18] And therefore will the Lord wait, that he may be gracious unto you, and therefore will he be exalted, that he may have mercy upon you: for the Lord is a God of judgment: blessed are all they that wait for him. [19] For the people shall dwell in Zion at Jerusalem: thou shalt weep no more: he will be very gracious unto thee at the voice of thy cry; when he shall hear it, he will answer

thee. ²⁰ And though the Lord give you the bread of adversity, and the water of affliction, yet shall not thy teachers be removed into a corner any more, but thine eyes shall see thy teachers: ²¹ And thine ears shall hear a word behind thee, saying, This is the way, walk ye in it, when ye turn to the right hand, and when ye turn to the left. ²² Ye shall defile also the covering of thy graven images of silver, and the ornament of thy molten images of gold: thou shalt cast them away as a menstruous cloth; thou shalt say unto it, Get thee hence. ²³ Then shall he give the rain of thy seed, that thou shalt sow the ground withal; and bread of the increase of the earth, and it shall be fat and plenteous: in that day shall thy cattle feed in large pastures. ²⁴ The oxen likewise and the young asses that ear the ground shall eat clean provender, which hath been winnowed with the shovel and with the fan. ²⁵ And there shall be upon every high mountain, and upon every high hill, rivers and streams of waters in the day of the great slaughter, when the towers fall. ²⁶ Moreover the light of the moon shall be as the light of the sun, and the light of the sun shall be sevenfold, as the light of seven days, in the day that the Lord bindeth up the breach of his people, and healeth the stroke of their wound. ²⁷ Behold, the name of the Lord cometh from far, burning with his anger, and the burden thereof is heavy: his lips are full of indignation, and his tongue as a devouring fire: ²⁸ And his breath, as an overflowing stream, shall reach to the midst of the neck, to sift the nations with the sieve of vanity: and there shall be a bridle in the jaws of the people, causing them to err. ²⁹ Ye shall have a song, as in the night when a holy solemnity is kept; and gladness of heart, as when one goeth with a pipe to come into the mountain of the Lord, to the mighty One of Israel. ³⁰ And the Lord shall cause his glorious voice to be heard, and shall shew the lighting down of his arm, with the indignation of his anger, and with the flame of a devouring fire, with scattering, and tempest, and hailstones. ³¹ For through the voice of the Lord shall the Assyrian be beaten down, which smote with a rod. ³² And in every place where the grounded staff shall pass, which the Lord shall lay upon him, it shall be with tabrets and harps: and in battles of shaking will he fight with it. ³³ For Tophet is ordained of old; yea, for the king it is prepared; he hath made it deep and large: the pile thereof is fire and much wood; the breath of the Lord, like a stream of brimstone, doth kindle it.

Isaiah 30:18-33

⁴ For thus hath the Lord spoken unto me, Like as the lion and the young lion roaring on his prey, when a multitude of shepherds is called forth against him, he will not be afraid of their voice, nor abase himself for the noise of them: so shall the Lord of hosts come down to

fight for mount Zion, and for the hill thereof. [5] As birds flying, so will the Lord of hosts defend Jerusalem; defending also he will deliver it; and passing over he will preserve it. [6] Turn ye unto him from whom the children of Israel have deeply revolted. [7] For in that day every man shall cast away his idols of silver, and his idols of gold, which your own hands have made unto you for a sin. [8] Then shall the Assyrian fall with the sword, not of a mighty man; and the sword, not of a mean man, shall devour him: but he shall flee from the sword, and his young men shall be discomfited. [9] And he shall pass over to his strong hold for fear, and his princes shall be afraid of the ensign, saith the Lord, whose fire is in Zion, and his furnace in Jerusalem.

Isaiah 31:4-9

To reiterate, the prophecies about the defeat of the king of Babylon and the Assyrian, who are one and the same and refer to the antichrist, are important because they anchor his time to a future time. They are important because they indicate his origin and future center of power is Iraq, for Iraq possesses the ruins of the capitals of both Assyria and Babylon, specifically the cities of Nineveh and Babylon, respectively. Shades of the Nimrod typology discussed in previous chapters can be seen here, for Nimrod, that first, wicked, world ruler, founded Babel (Babylon).

Part 3 – Alternate Theories

I now want to discuss alternate theories that the antichrist will come from Turkey, Syria, US, or Rome. I briefly addressed the Turkish theory in Chapter 1, and I dealt with the Turkish theory more extensively in <u>Is the United States Mentioned in Bible</u> <u>Prophecy? With a Treatise on the Ezekiel 38 and Psalm 83 Wars</u>, so I don't want to spend too much time covering old ground. Nevertheless, a short recounting of the major points to refute the Turkish theory is in order here.

The major argument that the Turkish theorists make is that the war of Ezekiel 38-39 in which Gog, i.e., the leader of Magog, and his allies invade Israel is a Tribulation war and that Magog is the ancient equivalent of modern Turkey, with Gog as its antichrist leader. The Turkish theorists go to great lengths to "prove" that Magog in ancient times was located in Asia Minor, or what we now know as Turkey. This theory entirely ignores the much larger and much more lethal Russia just to Turkey's north; in fact, the theorists go to great lengths to "prove" that Russia is not Magog.

To begin with, the war of Ezekiel 38-39 is a precursor war to the Tribulation and sets the stage for the rise of the antichrist. The second beast of Daniel 7 is the bear with three ribs in its mouth, being Russia in consort with Turkey, Syria, and Iran. Taken from my above-referenced book:

A November 5, 2007 online article by the Fars News Agency of Tehran (Fars is a province in Iran and is derived from the ancient name the Persians called their homeland, Parsa, which is retained in the term "Pars" or "Fars," from which the name of their language, "Farsi," is derived) had the headline, "Inevitable Iran-Turkey-Syria-Russia Alliance" and ended with, "The final effect of the region's aversion to American policies will be the formation of the "union of four:" Russia, Turkey, Iran and Syria. Of course, this rapprochement between Ankara, Moscow, Damascus and Tehran will definitely affect Washington's position in the Middle East." Without them knowing the prophetical implications, it appears that the Iranians have identified for us the three ribs in the bear's mouth.

During the writing of this book, on July 5, 2019, the Jerusalem Post published an article entitled "Turkey Announces 'Trilateral Summit' on Syria with Russia and Iran" that supports this truth. We see the dynamic of these four nations now, yet the majority of the Body of Christ is oblivious to it, and the theologians and prophecy scholars continue to view the bear beast of Daniel 7 as the ancient Medo-Persian empire. There is much more supporting information from the news headlines to demonstrate that the Russians are in cahoots with the Turks, Syrians, and Iranians and form the basis of the bear with three ribs in its mouth of Daniel 7. This bear with three ribs and other nations besides these four will invade Israel and be destroyed:

> [21] And I will call for a sword against him throughout all my mountains, saith the Lord God: every man's sword shall be against his brother. [22] And I will plead against him with pestilence and with blood; and I will rain upon him, and upon his bands, and upon the many people that are with him, an overflowing rain, and great hailstones, fire, and brimstone.

Ezekiel 38:21-22

In my book covering the Ezekiel 38-39 war, I show 14 points of difference between this war and the Tribulation wars. Although the language of Ezekiel 38-39 has some similarities to language in both the OT and NT regarding the Tribulation, these 14 points demonstrate that the Ezekiel 38-39 war **cannot** be a Tribulation war. On top of this, ancient historians record for us who they considered to be Magog and where he existed geographically. Again, pulling from my book:

> It is possible to examine some of these ancient sources and link them together to get a picture of who the Magogites' descendants are. We will examine three ancient sources: Herodotus, the Greek world traveler and historian who lived in the 5th century B.C.; Josephus, the 1st century A.D. Jewish historian; and Claudius Ptolemy, the Greco-Egyptian writer and mathematician

of the 2nd century A.D. We will begin with Herodotus, who introduces us to the Scythians.

Herodotus, Book IV: 20

Callippidae on the north coast of the Black Sea, beyond [which] is a mixed race part Scythian and part Greek; beyond them is a people named Alazones. Both these follow the Scythian way of life. Beyond these are Scythians who till and sow, not for food, but for sale. Beyond them are the Neuri and to the northward of those the land is uninhabited as far as we know.

Ptolemy expands our understanding of the Scythians.

Ptolemy, Book 2, Chapter 2: Of the Characteristics of the Inhabitants of the General Climes

Those who live under the more northern parallels, those, I mean, who have the **Bears** [Please note the reference to bears, i.e., Ursa Major/Ursa Minor, Big Dipper/Little Dipper] *over their heads, since they are far removed from the zodiac and the heat of the sun, are therefore cooled; but because they have a richer share of moisture, which is most nourishing and is not there exhausted by heat, they are white in complexion, straight-haired, tall and well-nourished, and somewhat cold by nature; these too are savage in their habits because their dwelling-places are continually cold. The wintry character of their climate, the size of their plants, and the* *wildness of their animals are in accord with these qualities. We call these men, too, by a general name, Scythians.*

Josephus connects the dots for us.

Flavius Josephus, Antiquities of the Jews, Book 1, Chapter 6:1

Magog founded those that from him were named Magogites, but who are by the Greeks called Scythians.

Therefore, the Scythians were descendants of Magog who lived in cold, northern climates - certainly north of the Black Sea, which itself is to the north of modern Turkey - and had fair skin and straight hair. Sounds like Russians to me.

I hope this will put the final nail in the coffin of the Turkish theory within the minds of my reading audience.

We can now examine the Syrian theory by examining Daniel 8.

[1] In the third year of the reign of king Belshazzar a vision appeared unto me, even unto me Daniel, after that which appeared unto me at the first. [2] And I saw in a vision; and it came to pass, when I saw, that I was at Shushan in the palace, which is in the province of Elam; and I saw in a vision, and I was by the river of Ulai. [3] Then I lifted up mine eyes, and saw, and, behold, there stood before the river a ram which had two horns: and the two horns were high; but one was higher than the other, and the

higher came up last [the Medo-Persian empire, in which the Persians became the dominant member over time]. [4] I saw the ram pushing westward, and northward, and southward; so that no beasts might stand before him, neither was there any that could deliver out of his hand; but he did according to his will, and became great. [5] And as I was considering, behold, an he goat [male goat] came from the west on the face of the whole earth, and touched not the ground: and the goat had a notable horn between his eyes [Alexander the Great]. [6] And he came to the ram that had two horns, which I had seen standing before the river, and ran unto him in the fury of his power. [7] And I saw him come close unto the ram, and he was moved with choler against him, and smote the ram, and brake his two horns: and there was no power in the ram to stand before him, but he cast him down to the ground, and stamped upon him: and there was none that could deliver the ram out of his hand. [8] Therefore the he goat waxed very great: and when he was strong, the great horn was broken; and for it came up four notable ones [Seleucus, Ptolemy, Lysimachus, and Cassander] toward the four winds of heaven. [9] And out of one of them came forth a little horn [the antichrist], which waxed exceeding great, toward the south, and toward the east, and toward the pleasant land [Israel, to the west]. [10] And it waxed great, even to the host of heaven;

and it cast down some of the host and of the stars to the ground, and stamped upon them. [11] Yea, he magnified himself even to the prince [Jesus] of the host, and by him the daily sacrifice was taken away, and the place of the sanctuary was cast down.

Daniel 8:1-11

This basis of this theory is that one of the four horns that sprung from Alexander after he died represents the people group from which the antichrist will come, particularly the Seleucids. One of the horns was Seleucus, one of the four generals who split up Alexander's empire. At the end of their reign, the Seleucids were mostly confined to Syria, which is the reason for proposing that the antichrist will come from Syria. But why the Seleucids? Well, one especially nasty Seleucid king, probably the nastiest one of all, was Antiochus Epiphanes. This wicked king is believed to serve as a model, or pre-type, of the antichrist, for historians tell us that that he went into the temple in Jerusalem and sacrificed a pig on the altar, which in turn caused the Jews, rightfully so, to go apoplectic and rise up in revolt through the Maccabees. Even his name betrays his lunacy, for he minted a coin on which he termed himself *theos epiphanes*, or "manifest god," and he was even mocked during his time with the name *Epimanes*, or "mad one." All that sounds reasonable for why Syria is selected as a candidate for the antichrist's origin, but the problem is that it ignores the fact that Seleucus began his reign from...guess where...wait for it...hold on...

Babylon. Scholars tell us that the Seleucid kings were called "kings of Babylon."

Note that Daniel 8:9 says the little horn (antichrist) will wax great (meaning get much bigger in conquered territory) toward the south, east, and west toward the "pleasant land," another name for Israel. If he will be Syrian, it is hard to see how he will "wax great" westward toward tiny Israel, since Syria already abuts the eastern border of Israel roughly along the same 35 degree, 33 minute longitudinal meridian east of the Prime Meridian in the Demilitarized Zone, and Syria borders the Mediterranean Sea as a western boundary condition. Also, why mention moving south without the phrase "toward the pleasant land," since Israel is also south of Syria? Furthermore, Damascus will have been "taken away from being a city" (Isaiah 17:1), and Syria itself will have been ruined by either the Ezekiel 38-39 war or the Psalm 83 war.

However, if he comes from Iraq, then the verse makes sense in that he will "wax great" south to Arabia and areas across the Red Sea into northeastern Africa (Egypt, Libya, Ethiopia – Daniel 11:43), east to Iran and beyond, and west through Jordan and Syria into Israel; nothing much going on north of him, since, remember, the Russians and Turks will have been royally stomped by their foray into Israel, as Ezekiel

38-39 describe. Immediately south of Iraq is Saudi Arabia, indicating he will overtake the Saudis and control their territory, including Mecca. This is a bit off-topic for this chapter and perhaps is more suited to the following Muslim chapter, but he obviously will not make a big deal of Mecca, because his energies will be focused on Jerusalem, as Scripture makes abundantly clear. If he were wanting to make a big splash of being the Muslim Mahdi, it seems to me he would enter the Kaaba in the Grand Mosque of Mecca and declare himself to be sent from Allah and then move into Jerusalem, but I see no evidence of that in Scripture.

We now come to the theory that the US will be the origin of the antichrist or that, at a minimum, the US will be the power base of his kingdom. Searches on YouTube and the internet with terms like "United States prophecy" or "America prophecy" will lead to a slew of sites asserting that the US will be the fourth beast of Daniel 7 and/or that it is the beast of Revelation 13, with New York as the actual city of Babylon the Great of Revelation 17 and 18. Some of these sites follow the British Israelism theory, that the US is an offshoot of the British and is filled with descendants of the ten Lost Tribes of Israel; one site I found likens US to Manasseh and the British to Ephraim, stating that these two nations fulfill Israel's prophecies about Joseph and his sons in Genesis 49.

Many of these sites state that the US started off well but will transition into the Mystery Babylon harlot of Revelation

17, citing all the evils that the US manifests, such as rampant sexual immorality of all forms, including homosexuality, bestiality, sado-masochism, transgenderism, pornography, and pedophilia; substance abuse; gluttony; false religions and apostasy in the Church; satanism; divorce and breakdown of the family; corrupt government; feminism and cultural emasculation of males; and greed. I could go on. The proponents of the US-beast theory cite our global reach and military prowess as contributing factors to their thesis. One newsletter I received during the writing of this book terms US the Romerican Empire, with recitation of parallels between US and the histories of the Persians, Russians, Greeks, Romans, Germans, and British as the bases of this belief. Although I disagree with these various groups' positions regarding US as the antichrist's power base or as Mystery Babylon, at least I'm happy to see that there are people who believe the US is presented in Scripture, for there are some very well-known prophecy ministries who adamantly maintain the US cannot be found anywhere in Scripture. I vigorously oppose that position.

Now, on the flip side of the coin, those same searches on YouTube and the internet will lead you to another slew of sites asserting that dreams and visions by the owners of those sites indicate the US will suffer severe judgment and be destroyed before the rise of the antichrist. A common theme with relatively great consistency is attack by foreign enemies, specifically the Russians and Chinese, but the North Koreans get tossed in there occasionally as the culprits which lob nuclear missiles over US to cause electromagnetic pulse strikes that return US to the dark ages. Another common theme is massive natural disasters: earthquakes, volcanoes, tsunamis, fires, hurricanes, and gargantuan tornadoes. Accompanying these attacks and disasters are tales of martial law; FEMA concentration camps used as killing fields; anarchy and massive civil unrest and civil war; beheadings of Christians by the droves; etc., etc., and so on, and so on. David Wilkerson's The Vision prophecies and those of William Branham, A.A. Allen, Dimitru Duduman, Henry Gruver, Ken Peters, and others are typically proffered as supporting prophecies for these dreams and visions. Some propose that the following verses refer to destruction of the US and Western nations and thereby support these dreams and visions:

> Sheba, and Dedan [assumed to be Saudi Arabia in league with Western nations], and the merchants of Tarshish [supposedly modern Great Britain or western European nations], with all the young lions [the lions referring to the British, since that's their symbol, and all the former British colonies, including US] thereof, shall say unto thee, Art thou come to take a spoil?

> Ezekiel 38:13

And I will send a fire on Magog [Russia], and among
them that dwell carelessly in the isles [allegedly the UK
and former colonies, including US]: and they shall know
that I am the Lord.

Ezekiel 39:6

There is a great debate going on within the US Church
regarding whether God still speaks directly to His people
rather than only through Scripture. The opponents of the
direct-speaking approach attack "contemplative prayer" and
"centering prayer" and criticize anyone who claims to have
received a direct "word from the Lord," stating it smacks of
mysticism and is prone to satanic deception. I agree with many
of their positions, for I have seen numerous examples of the
phenomenon of someone claiming, "The Lord told me…," only
to find out the Lord said nothing of the sort, because their
proclamation did not pan out and led to rotten fruit. On the
other hand, to those who take the hardline position that God
no longer speaks to His people directly, I will take this
opportunity to remind them of the following:

[27] My sheep hear my voice [I feel relatively safe in saying
that this verse indicates that God still speaks to His
people; Jesus didn't put a timeline on it, as if it only
worked until the Apostle John died], and I know them,
and they follow me:

John 10:27

[17] And it shall come to pass in the last days [I feel relatively safe in saying that we're in the last days], saith God, I will pour out of my Spirit upon all flesh: and your sons and your daughters shall prophesy, and your young men shall see visions, and your old men shall dream dreams [I feel relatively safe in saying that God has to speak to these people in some way, shape, or form to transmit these dreams and visions]:

Acts 2:17

[26] Likewise the Spirit also helpeth our infirmities: for we know not what we should pray for as we ought: but the Spirit itself maketh intercession for us with groanings which cannot be uttered [I don't think it's too much of a stretch to propose that this is another way God communicates directly to us, if not by actual words or by Scripture, to get us moving in the right direction].

Romans 8:26

[7] But the manifestation of the Spirit is given to every man to profit withal. [8] For to one is given by the Spirit the word of wisdom; to another the word of knowledge [I feel like I'm on solid ground in saying that God somehow has to communicate this knowledge directly, for the word of knowledge is not a generic thing about knowledge but is knowledge about a specific thing hidden from others; God has revealed to other

Christians on several occasions things in my life that **nobody** else could have known for the purpose of teaching and encouraging me, and none of those personal revelations controverted Scripture] by the same Spirit; [9] To another faith by the same Spirit; to another the gifts of healing by the same Spirit; [10] To another the working of miracles; to another prophecy [OK, well, since the testimony of Jesus is the Spirit of prophecy, I feel like I'm on solid ground in saying that God has to speak to His people to transmit information about the future; the doctrine that prophecy died with the Apostle John is nowhere taught in Scripture, and as long as prophecies do not violate Scripture, they are not adding to Scripture and do not violate the warning of Revelation 22:18]; to another discerning of spirits; to another divers kinds of tongues; to another the interpretation of tongues [How can one interpret tongues unless God reveals the interpretation?]:

1 Corinthians 12:7-10

Since it is true that "the natural man receiveth not the things of the Spirit of God," but "he that is spiritual judgeth all things," then it indicates there must be a difference between us and the non-believer that has something to do with God imparting His thoughts to us. Wonder of wonders, there is a difference, for "we have the mind of Christ"! (1 Corinthians 2:14-16) The Holy Spirit living within us is not an inanimate

117

tool similar to a language translator software program that we grab at will to help us unlock Scripture in ways the lost cannot. Rather, He communicates actively with us to guide us into the truth, just as Jesus said: " Howbeit when he, the Spirit of truth, is come, he will guide you into all truth: for he shall not speak of himself; but whatsoever he shall hear, that shall he speak: and he will shew you things to come." (John 16:13) Did His mission of guiding us into truth, speaking to us, and showing us things to come stop at Apostle John's death? Of course not. Therefore, as dangerous and silly as this weird contemplative and centering prayer movement is, so also is the counter-movement to place constraints of communication on God and His people that are not taught in Scripture. As is so common for us, we flow to one side or the other of the road to the gutters of bad theology rather than straight down the middle of the road to truth where Jesus is.

Why did I go down that rabbit hole? I went down that rabbit hole because I believe the overwhelming number of dreams and visions showing consistency among them for extreme judgment on US before the antichrist arises dovetails perfectly with the Daniel 7 lion-eagle beast that has its wings plucked. God is communicating with His people, and He is doing so by communicating to us details not reported in Scripture but supported by Scripture. Given that God said He would give us dreams and visions in the last days, it necessitates that we see if we can match them up with

Scripture. It turns out that we can. The eagle of Daniel 7 is US, and we get our wings plucked as judgment for our wickedness as a nation. This happens before the Daniel 7 Russian bear with three ribs (Syria, Turkey, Iran) gets judged during its Ezekiel 38-39 attack on Israel. Our wings are plucked before the Daniel 7 Asian leopard beast arises and before the antichrist arises to form a global lion-bear-leopard amalgamation of the three predecessor beasts. These nations are the prominent nations in the news every day. Daniel 7 is happening before our eyes, yet the Church largely is blind to it and still clings to that old, incorrect, Babylon-Persia-Greece-Rome interpretation of Daniel 7.

Further to my opposition to the theory of the US as the beast's seat of power is that the proponents of it, much like the folks offering up names for the antichrist, over-rely on the US's wealth, power, influence, and wickedness as their proof that the US is Babylon. Some will go further and say that geographic and physiographic features (large cities and populations; various landforms including mountains, rivers, plains, and seas) of the US match descriptions of such features in Scripture, meaning that Scripture describes US in a physical manner. But they ignore the passages about Babylon's actual location and from where Scripture declares the antichrist will hail. As shown above, the antichrist will be Assyrian/Babylonian/Iraqi, not American. This leads to my final proof, beginning in the paragraph below.

I have selected a final passage to make my case that the antichrist will be Iraqi and, by doing so, I also will address the Rome theory. I often have wondered how the proponents of the Rome-is-Babylon (Mystery Babylon of Revelation) theory interpret the following passage in Zechariah.

> [1] Then I turned, and lifted up mine eyes, and looked, and behold a flying roll. [2] And he said unto me, What seest thou? And I answered, I see a flying roll; the length thereof is twenty cubits, and the breadth thereof ten cubits. [3] Then said he unto me, This is the curse that goeth forth over the face of the whole earth: for every one that stealeth shall be cut off as on this side according to it; and every one that sweareth shall be cut off as on that side according to it. [4] I will bring it forth, saith the Lord of hosts, and it shall enter into the house of the thief, and into the house of him that sweareth falsely by my name: and it shall remain in the midst of his house, and shall consume it with the timber thereof and the stones thereof. [5] Then the angel that talked with me went forth, and said unto me, Lift up now thine eyes, and see what is this that goeth forth. [6] And I said, What is it? And he said, This is an ephah [basket] that goeth forth. He said moreover, This is their resemblance through all the earth. [7] And, behold, there was lifted up a talent of lead: and this is a woman [Mystery Babylon, the harlot of Revelation 17] that sitteth in the midst of the ephah.

8 And he said, This is wickedness. And he cast it into the midst of the ephah; and he cast the weight of lead upon the mouth thereof. 9 Then lifted I up mine eyes, and looked, and, behold, there came out two women, and the wind was in their wings; for they had wings like the wings of a stork: and they lifted up the ephah between the earth and the heaven. 10 Then said I to the angel that talked with me, Whither do these bear the ephah? 11 And he said unto me, To build it an house in the **land of Shinar** [the alluvial plains of Shinar is where Babylon exists]: and it shall be established, and set there upon **her** [a female, as in "MYSTERY, BABYLON THE GREAT, THE MOTHER OF HARLOTS AND ABOMINATIONS OF THE EARTH" (Revelation 17:5)] base.

Zechariah 5

The Rome-is-Babylon folks promote the Pope-is-the-antichrist theory that gained prominence during and after the Protestant Reformation, even to modern times. Rooms could be stacked floor to ceiling with writings of various types claiming that the Pope is the antichrist and that his capital will be Rome. Some prophecy proponents claim that the Babylon of Revelation is a code word for Rome, the City of Seven Hills, citing the mention of seven mountains in Revelation 17:9 as proof. Nonsense. We again need to employ Occam's razor to this. I would ask, how were the readers of Revelation down through history supposed to know this insider's secret meaning of Babylon as Rome (or, as some insist, New York)? Why not just start with the way we do most literature and take it at face value that Babylon means Babylon, that place of infamy in the land of Shinar that God cursed many times in the OT; Rome is nowhere mentioned in the OT. Paul had no problem mentioning Rome when he meant Rome, and Peter had no problem mentioning Babylon when he meant Babylon. Both Paul and Peter died in Rome, and Peter went to Babylon in his ministry to the Jews who had chosen to remain there after their national, 70-year Babylonian captivity.

Part 4 – In Summation

Here is the issue: Babylon will be rebuilt in the end times as the headquarters of the Mother of Harlots from Revelation 17, the false religious system that first raised its ugly head under Nimrod, the prototype of the final antichrist. I have said in other books that parallels, patterns, and pre-types teach precepts, principles, and prophecies. One pattern is that God tends to revisit things to bring His purposes to completion, or He has parallel actions that we first see in the OT and then see again in the NT. In 1 Corinthians, Paul saw this principle of patterns in the 12 Tribes' wanderings in the wilderness and said it serves as an example for us in the last days. With respect to Babylon, God allowed the pantheistic, anti-God world system to start in Babylon under Nimrod, the pre-type of the antichrist, and He will destroy the antichrist's pantheistic, anti-God world system in Babylon. Thus, I appreciate those students of prophecy who have come out in recent years to point out that the Bible is Middle Eastern-centric, not European-centric, and that we've spent way too much mental energy thinking about Europe rather than where most of the Biblical action occurs, i.e., the Middle East. The Biblical narrative started in the Middle East, and it will end in the Middle East. Therefore, because the antichrist's capital will be in Babylon, i.e., modern Iraq, it is reasonable to believe that he will come from Iraq.

Chapter 11

MUSLIM

I spent some effort in Chapters 1 and 10 deconstructing the idea that the antichrist will be from Turkey and that he distinctly will be Muslim leading Muslim hordes against Israel. There is more about the Muslim angle that I want to address now that I felt would have been too unwieldy to address in previous chapters. One of the facts that speaks against the antichrist being strictly Muslim leading Muslim armies is that the Muslim armies will have been wiped out in the wars of Ezekiel 38-39 and Psalm 83. I dealt with these two wars in detail in Is the United States Mentioned in Bible Prophecy? With a Treatise on the Ezekiel 38 and Psalm 83 Wars. My position was then and remains now that the Russians and their Islamic allies will be defeated before the antichrist ascends to power and, in fact, pave the way for his ascendancy. To reiterate from Chapter 10, these wars are pre-Tribulation wars and fit the pattern of the four beasts of Daniel

7, one of which is the Russian bear with three ribs in its mouth consisting of Turkey, Syria, and Iran. This bear wanes in power and is replaced by the Asian leopard with four heads and four wings, which probably represent China, the Koreas, Japan, and India, although two heads could be separate Korean heads without India, or maybe India could be replaced with the all the other nations of southeast Asia and the Pacific Rim.

In any case, the Muslim nations aligned with Russia in Ezekiel 38-39 and those Muslim nations of Psalm 83 touching Israel's borders will be defeated before the antichrist rises to power, so that Islam will be removed as a major influence by the time he arrives on the scene. This is fitting, for the Muslims are uncontrollable and will need to be tamed to fall in line with his agenda. Remember, Scripture says he will worship himself above all other gods, such that the Muslim god will not hold his allegiance.

Nevertheless, in Chapter 1 I left myself an out by saying that I believe he will have a Muslim component to his overall complexion. I have no direct, Scriptural reference for this, but it is impossible to ignore his Iraqi nativity, since Iraq is predominantly Muslim. It also follows that, given his need to appeal to the masses, it will be convenient for him to point to his Muslim background and fool the Muslims about his loyalties as well as the Jews and Christians. He will be the great, false unifier of the Abrahamic religions, the three major religions that are mono-theistic. Therefore, based on that premise, I propose that he will have a Muslim upbringing, or at least come from that cultural milieu.

Chapter 12

CHRISTIAN CULTURAL INFLUENCE

I watched with considerable interest the game that Barack Obama played with the evangelical Christian community during his rise to power and during his tenure as president. To the spiritually discerning eye, this man is a godless pretender who used the Christian community, at least gullible portions of it, to accomplish his wicked objectives. He slipped up in an interview with ABC's George Stephanopoulos with the snippet "my Muslim faith"; his biological father was Muslim in his youth (then died as an atheist); his stepfather was Muslim; his half-brother is Muslim and has been linked to Islamic radicals; and he bowed to the Saudi king, the steward of Mecca, which no other US president has done. But the American citizenry was not yet ready for a Muslim president, or at least one sympathetic to Islam, so what better way to ingratiate yourself to a large portion of the American populace than to belly up to a Christian denomination and play Christian?

Many Christians bought into it hook, line, and sinker and helped propel this impostor forward, enabling him to place pro-abortion, pro-LGBTQ jurists on the Supreme Court and usher in homosexuality and transgenderism as norms, all the while attacking Israel in the arena of public opinion. He attacked Christianity whenever it turned out to be the low-hanging fruit to pick (on) and turned a blind eye to the evils of Islam.

If the antichrist was also watching it – assuming he is alive at this time – then he may have gotten some tips on how to hoodwink Christians. Recall that Jesus said in Matthew 24:24, "For there shall arise false Christs, and false prophets, and shall shew great signs and wonders; insomuch that, **if it were possible**, they shall deceive the very elect." Christians won't ultimately be deceived by the antichrist, but Jesus leaves the door open to the idea that Christians certainly are susceptible to deception.

It is in the same vein as the previous chapter on the antichrist being Muslim that I propose he may also identify himself as a Christian. Perhaps he is raised in Iraq by a Muslim father, making him Muslim by faith, and by a Jewish mother, making him a Jew by blood, but then he goes off to school or finds a job in Europe or America and gets exposed to cultural Christianity. A man for all seasons and cultures and religions.

I have no direct Scriptural proof of this theory, yet it makes sense from a common-sense approach and by the example of Obama. One final thought: the history of cults such as Gnostics, Arians, Jehovah's Witnesses, Mormons, Peoples Temple, Branch Davidians, and so on is that they were all founded by men who came out of orthodox Christian backgrounds, or who at least were heavily exposed to Christian orthodoxy. I see no reason to think it can't happen the same way with the antichrist.

Chapter 13

NO REGARD FOR WOMEN

[37] Neither shall he regard the God of his fathers, nor the desire of women, nor regard any god: for he shall magnify himself above all. [38] But in his estate shall he honour the God of forces: and a god whom his fathers knew not shall he honor with gold, and silver, and with precious stones, and pleasant things. [39] Thus shall he do in the most strong holds with a strange god, whom he shall acknowledge and increase with glory: and he shall cause them to rule over many, and shall divide the land for gain.

Daniel 11:37-39

The usual commentary on these verses is that the antichrist will be a homosexual. Perhaps he will be, since he will be a perversion of everything that God has said is good, which includes heterosexual marriage. But the verse doesn't state that; it simply says he will have no regard for the desire

of women, not that he won't have any desire **for** women. It's that which women desire for which he has no regard. The previous sentence leads to another theory, that the phrase "desire of women" is an allusion to Jewish women wanting to be the mother of the Messiah, which then follows that he will have no regard for Jesus. However, my readings on this theory indicate that the desire of Jewish women to be the mother of the Messiah is not well supported in Jewish Bible commentaries (midrashim and targumim) and literature. Another theory is that, since the history of Israel's kings show that their pagan wives led them into idolatry, perhaps this is a way of saying that the antichrist will have no concern for the idols of his women, assuming he has women, or of any woman. Maybe his upbringing in a Muslim environment will have prepped him for this mindset, since women generally are not held in high esteem in much of Muslim culture. Given that the context of the verse is about his disregard for any gods, perhaps his lack of concern for the idols of his women is the correct interpretation.

Irrespective of the above theories, this guy is the supreme MGTOW, or mig-tow (rhymes with pig-cow), as in Men Going Their Own Way. For those of you not familiar with this growing men's movement, it is the destructive, unproductive response to feminism of a small segment of Western, or westernized, heterosexual males who have voluntarily sworn off interaction with women to varying degrees, because they find women increasingly repulsive in behavior. As for the beast, his reason for having no interest in the things of women might have nothing to do with his sexual preference or whether he perceives women as repulsive, but rather it will be that he has no interest in anything or anyone other than the "god of forces" of Daniel 11:38 and himself. He will be the ultimate, human narcissist, his dad being the only one who surpasses him in narcissism.

Chapter 14

UTTERLY EVIL

This is a no-brainer, some in the reading audience must be thinking, so why present it as a characteristic that needs to be unlocked through careful, deductive reasoning about the relevant Scriptures? My answer is that I want to impress upon the reader just how evil this man will be and just how much damage he will do to the whole world, most directly to the Body of Christ and God's chosen nation, Israel. Again, it goes back to my mission to warn the Body of Christ about the impending holocaust.

Examining the relevant Scriptures about the antichrist, we find that he will be entirely lawless, deceitful, untruthful, unholy, occultic, hedonistic, narcissistic, and blood-thirsty, meaning he will recognize no boundaries for human behavior and will have no regard for human life; he will purposely mislead people; he will be a liar; he will be ritually unclean; he will consort with demonic realms; he will mindlessly pursue filthy, vile physical pleasures; he will be supremely self-absorbed; and he will take pleasure in murder. He will be the most despicable, profane, wicked human to ever exist, and his intent will be to destroy Jesus and His Body, which also means he will be the most delusional human to ever live. A chip off the Old Block, the most self-deceived creature to ever live. Two supporting passages are presented below, but there are many more.

> [1] Now we beseech you, brethren, by the coming of our Lord Jesus Christ, and by our gathering together unto him, [2] That ye be not soon shaken in mind, or be troubled, neither by spirit, nor by word, nor by letter as from us, as that the day of Christ is at hand. [3] Let no man deceive you by any means: for that day shall not come, except there come a falling away first, and that man of sin be revealed, the son of perdition; [4] Who opposeth and exalteth himself above all that is called God, or that is worshipped; so that he as God sitteth in the temple of God, shewing himself that he is God. [5] Remember ye not, that, when I was yet with you, I told you these things? [6] And now ye know what withholdeth that he might be revealed in his time. [7] For the mystery of iniquity doth already work: only he who now letteth will let, until he be taken out of the way. [8] And then shall that Wicked be revealed, whom the Lord shall consume with the spirit of his mouth, and shall destroy with the brightness of his

coming: [9] Even him, whose coming is after the working of Satan with all power and signs and lying wonders, [10] And with all deceivableness of unrighteousness in them that perish; because they received not the love of the truth, that they might be saved.

2 Thessalonians 2:1-10

[19] And I saw the beast, and the kings of the earth, and their armies, gathered together to make war against him that sat on the horse [Jesus], and against his army [the Body of Christ].

Revelation 19:19

You would have to have a special type of irrationality, mindlessness, and arrogance to take on the Living Lord of Glory and His armies; thus, it is fitting that Peter speaks of these types of people, among them the antichrist, and what will happen to them:

[12] But these, as natural brute beasts [It is appropriate that the antichrist also is called the beast], made to be taken and destroyed, speak evil of the things that they understand not; and shall utterly perish in their own corruption;

2 Peter 2:12

Scripture records that the beast will have a special animus toward Christians and Jews. Christians will be hunted down and killed though various means and methods, including decapitation (Revelation 20:4). The antichrist-is-Muslim proponents use the decapitation phenomenon as an argument for the antichrist being Muslim, but considering that multitudes of cultures and religions have used this method of execution for millennia, I don't put any stock in that argument. But the point is made: he will be an insanely malevolent dictator who will rain unholy, excruciatingly painful fire down on the people of God, either figuratively or literally (Revelation 13:13).

Now, I know that many in the reading audience will think to themselves, "No problem, I won't be here anyway to experience the Tribulation, since I'm getting raptured out of here before the really bad stuff happens." To that I say, I greatly urge you to reconsider your position, because the pre-Tribulation rapture doctrine is a false doctrine and one that has caused many Christians to become complacent and in violation of Christ's command to always watch current events and watch for His second coming. There is also a subtle form of pride and disconnection from reality, for that belief reveals gross ignorance of the atrocities already being committed against millions of Christians around the world that rival any level of suffering Christians will endure during the Tribulation. The false hope of a pre-Trib rapture provides no value to a Christian being beheaded by ISIS or starving to death in a North Korean concentration camp. Their tribulation is **now**.

The sad fact is that many, many Christians will be utterly unprepared for the Tribulation because of their false belief that they will sit the Tribulation out in heaven. They and the pre-Trib prophecy "experts" do not understand the feasts/high holy days of Israel and how the last three feasts/high holy days – Trumpets (the rapture), Day of Atonement, and Tabernacles – will be fulfilled in the final days of the Tribulation in the same way that Jesus fulfilled the first four feasts/high holy days – Passover, Unleavened Bread, First Fruits, and Pentecost – during His first advent, i.e., in consecutive order following the same date patterns over a few days to weeks, as outlined in the OT. Time and space do not permit me to address this issue in detail here, but for anyone who cares, I address the details in The Timing of the Rapture. I also briefly deal with the topic of the rapture in Chapter 15.

I have encountered numerous Christians – obviously not all – who I would describe as spiritually numbed down and dumbed down as a direct result of this laissez faire attitude toward the Tribulation and its primary antagonist, the antichrist; I have heard their apathy straight from their mouths and observed it in their behavior, even as I have been guilty of the same in times past. I vehemently espoused the pre-Trib rapture position for 18 years until I threw out all the commentaries and books (in a figurative sense) and started from scratch to come to my current, equally-vehement position that the Church will not be raptured until near the end of the

Tribulation on the Feast of Trumpets, nine Days before Atonement and fourteen days before Tabernacles. It is imperative that Christians get the message that an early understanding and identification of the antichrist will help them prepare for the coming persecution. There needs to be some fear in Christians, a healthy fear like Noah had that compelled him to make all necessary preparations for the cleansing Flood.

> [7] By faith Noah, being warned of God of things not seen as yet, **moved with fear**, prepared an ark to the saving of his house; by the which he condemned the world, and became heir of the righteousness which is by faith.

> Hebrews 11:7

Joseph had a similar mindset when he prepared for seven years of famine by storing up grain the prior seven years. It is evident with these two catastrophes – flood and famine – that God's method has been one of taking His people **through** the tribulations, not out of them.

> [15] I [Jesus] pray **not that thou shouldest take them out of the world**, but that thou shouldest keep them from the evil.

> John 17:15

My desire and prayer are that Christians will take to heart the issues presented herein and act upon them. Prophecy was designed by God to light a way for us to see the otherwise hidden glories and dangers to know how to properly respond when these events occur.

> [19] We have also a more sure word of prophecy; whereunto ye do well that ye take heed, as unto a light that shineth in a dark place, until the day dawn, and the day star arise in your hearts:

2 Peter 1:19

Therefore, I urge readers to take the "more sure word of prophecy" and be wise, for to do otherwise would be foolish and deadly.

> [3] A prudent man foreseeth the evil, and hideth himself: but the simple pass on, and are punished.

Proverbs 22:3

Chapter 15

LOOK UP

^{28} And when these things begin to come to pass, then look up, and lift up your heads; for your redemption draweth nigh.

Luke 21:28

The antichrist's reign is a double-edged sword. One edge of the sword is horrific and leads to the greatest carnage the world will ever know, but the other edge leads to the greatest victory the world will ever know: the defeat of Satan and his seed combined with the return of Jesus. While the world will be crushed with despair during the antichrist's reign of terror, the believer can be filled with hope for the coming reign of Jesus, the Lord of Glory. Following the defeat of the antichrist and his forces at the Battle of Armageddon, Jesus will enter the east gate of the fourth temple and begin His millennial reign. I say fourth temple, accounting that Solomon's was the first; Ezra's was the second; the Tribulation temple of Revelation

11:1-2 will be the third (actually, it will be more like the tabernacle of the Jews' 40-year wilderness wanderings, based on the Greek words *naon* and *naos* used by Paul and John to describe this temple as a small structure); and the temple of Ezekiel 40-43 built by Jesus will be the fourth. Once Jesus is enthroned in the fourth temple, His millennial reign will be filled with abundance – peace, righteousness, justice, equity, and intolerance for rebellion.

Presented in the following passages in chronological order by future event are passages of Scripture that describe our Lord's activities in the final days of the Tribulation leading into His millennial reign. We will begin with Tishri 1, which historically was known as the Feast of Trumpets but is now known as Rosh Hashanah, or the Head of the Year, meaning the beginning of the Jewish year. This feast has a September/October timeframe under our modern calendar and, in some future year, will coincide with the rapture of the Church. Tishri 1/Trumpets initiates the ten-day period called by the Jews the Days of Awe leading to Tishri 10, which is the Day of Atonement wherein the Jews "shall look upon me [Jesus] whom they have pierced, and they shall mourn for him..." Following Tishri 10/Atonement is Tishri 15, which is the beginning of the Feast of Tabernacles, signifying the beginning of the thousand-year period in which Jesus will tabernacle, or dwell, with the believing Jew and Gentile survivors of the Tribulation; these survivors will get saved sometime between Tishri 1 and Tishri 15, after the rapture but before the Battle of Armageddon, a.k.a. the Day of the Lord.

Tishri 1 – Trumpets/Rapture

The OT provides the model for the prophecies concerning Jesus's earthly ministry and His heavenly ministry leading up to His return, as seen in the seven feasts of Israel described in Leviticus 23. Jesus fulfilled the first four feasts of Israel in consecutive, chronological order on the Jewish calendar over an approximate seven and one-half-week period in the spring to early summer – Passover, Unleavened Bread, First Fruits, and Pentecost, signifying the first plantings of believers in the spring to the first harvest of believers in early summer – and will fulfill over an approximate two-week period the final three feasts that cover the fall's final harvest of believers – Trumpets, Atonement, and Tabernacles. For this discussion, we will begin with Trumpets, which commemorates the Exodus 19 meeting between the Lord and the Israelites in which the Lord descended from the mountain in a cloud, a trumpet was blown, and the people came up to the foot of the mountain to meet the Lord. Sound familiar? It perfectly describes its NT counterpart, the rapture. The requisite passages describing Trumpets/rapture are as follows:

[29] Immediately **after the tribulation** [folks, **after** really does mean after, not pre-] of those days shall the sun be darkened, and the moon shall not give her light, and the

stars shall fall from heaven, and the powers of the heavens shall be shaken: [30] And then shall appear the sign of the Son of man [Jesus] in heaven: and then shall all the tribes of the earth mourn, and they shall see the Son of man coming in the clouds of heaven with power and great glory. [31] And he shall send his angels with a great **sound of a trumpet** [the seventh trumpet of Revelation 10:7, wherein the mystery of God (the rapture) should be finished] and **they shall gather together his elect from the four winds, from one end of heaven to the other** ["the dead in Christ shall rise first," 1 Thessalonians 4:16].

Matthew 24:29-31

[24] But in those days, **after that tribulation,** the sun shall be darkened, and the moon shall not give her light, [25] And the stars of heaven shall fall, and the powers that are in heaven shall be shaken. [26] And then shall they see the Son of man coming in the clouds with great power and glory. [26] And then shall they see the Son of man coming in the clouds with great power and glory. [27] And then shall he send his angels, and **shall gather together his elect from the four winds, from the uttermost part of the earth** ["Then we which are alive and remain shall be caught up together with them in the clouds, to meet the Lord in the air," (1 Thessalonians 4:17)] **to the**

148

uttermost part of heaven [which captures the dead in Christ].

Mark 13:24-27

[51] Behold, I shew you a **mystery** [the same one as that of Revelation 10:7, wherein the mystery of God (the rapture) should be finished]; We shall not all sleep, but we shall all be changed, [52] In a moment, in the twinkling of an eye, at the last **trump** [the seventh trumpet of Revelation 10:7]: for the **trumpet** shall sound, and **the dead shall be raised incorruptible** [meaning raptured], and we shall be changed.

1 Corinthians 15:51-52

[14] For if we believe that Jesus died and rose again, even so them also which sleep [the dead in Christ, the elect in heaven of Matthew 24:31 and Mark 13:27] in Jesus will God bring with him. [15] For this we say unto you by the word of the Lord, that we which are alive and remain [those who will not sleep, i.e., the elect from the uttermost part of earth of Mark 13:27] unto the coming of the Lord shall not prevent them which are asleep. [16] For the Lord himself shall descend from heaven with a shout, with the voice of the archangel, and with the **trump** [the seventh trumpet of Revelation 10:7, the one announcing the completion of the mystery of 1 Corinthians 15:51, i.e., the rapture] of God: and the dead

in Christ shall rise first:[17] Then we which are alive and remain shall be caught up together with them in the clouds, to meet the Lord in the air: and so shall we ever be with the Lord.

1 Thessalonians 4:14-17

[7] But in the days of the voice of the seventh angel, when he shall begin to **sound** [his trumpet, the seventh], the **mystery** of God [the same mystery as that of 1 Corinthians 15:51, meaning the rapture] should be finished, as he hath declared to his servants the prophets.

Revelation 10:7

[14] And I looked, and behold a white cloud, and upon the cloud one sat like unto the Son of man [Jesus], having on his head a golden crown, and in his hand a sharp sickle. [15] And another angel came out of the temple, crying with a loud voice to him that sat on the cloud, Thrust in thy sickle, and reap: for the time is come for thee to reap; for the harvest of the earth is ripe. [16] And he that sat on the cloud thrust in his sickle on the earth; and the earth was reaped [the rapture, the harvesting of the wheat, mirroring the parable of the wheat and tares in Matthew 13:24-43].

Revelation 14:14-16

Tishri 1 of an unknown, future year will be a very busy day, for it will lead to the marriage of the Bridegroom to His Bride.

> [7] Let us be glad and rejoice, and give honour to him: for the marriage of the Lamb is come, and his wife hath made herself ready. [8] And to her was granted that she should be arrayed in fine linen, clean and white: for the fine linen is the righteousness of saints.

> Revelation 19:7-8

Following the marriage, the heavens will open up and the world will see the glorious Bridegroom and His resplendent Bride.

> [11] And I saw heaven opened, and behold a white horse; and he that sat upon him was called Faithful and True, and in righteousness he doth judge and make war. [12] His eyes were as a flame of fire, and on his head were many crowns; and he had a name written, that no man knew, but he himself. [13] And he was clothed with a vesture dipped in blood [which connects this to Isaiah 63:1-6, to be discussed below]: and his name is called The Word of God. [14] And the armies [meaning us, His Bride] which were in heaven followed him upon white horses, clothed in fine linen, white and clean.

> Revelation 19:11-14

Among those who will see the Bridegroom and His Bride will be the Jews. It will cause great consternation of the soul and great remorse that they missed Him the first time. This brings us to Tishri 10.

Tishri 10 - Atonement

[10] And I will pour upon the house of David, and upon the inhabitants of Jerusalem, the spirit of grace and of supplications: and they shall look upon me whom they have pierced, and they shall mourn for him, as one mourneth for his only son, and shall be in bitterness for him, as one that is in bitterness for his firstborn. [11] In that day shall there be a great mourning in Jerusalem, as the mourning of Hadadrimmon in the valley of Megiddon [Note the reference to the valley of Meggidon, or Armageddon of Revelation 16:16, also known as the valley of decision of Joel 3:14]. [12] And the land shall mourn, every family apart; the family of the house of David [kings/rulers] apart, and their wives apart; the family of the house of Nathan [prophets] apart, and their wives apart; [13] The family of the house of Levi [priests] apart, and their wives apart; the family of Shimei [commoners] apart, and their wives apart; [14] All the families that remain, every family apart, and their wives apart.

Zechariah 12:10-14

At that time, the Jews truly will do what was ordained of old for them to do, to mourn for their sins, to "afflict" their souls.

> ²⁹ And this shall be a statute for ever unto you: that in the seventh month, on the tenth day of the month, ye shall **afflict your souls**, and do no work at all, whether it be one of your own country, or a stranger that sojourneth among you:

> Leviticus 16:29

Sometime between Tishri 10 and Tishri 15, Jesus will gather the Jews hidden in modern Jordan, known as Edom, Moab, and Ammon in times past. Daniel and Revelation, when linked together to get the full picture, confirm that the majority of Jews (some will remain in Jerusalem) will escape the antichrist by fleeing to Jordan.

> ⁴¹ He [antichrist] shall enter also into the glorious land, and many countries shall be overthrown: but these shall escape out of his hand, even Edom, and Moab, and the chief of the children of Ammon [modern Jordan].

> Daniel 11:41

> ¹ And there appeared a great wonder in heaven; a woman clothed with the sun, and the moon under her feet, and upon her head a crown of twelve stars: [the nation of Israel] ² And she being with child cried,

travailing in birth, and pained to be delivered. ³ And there appeared another wonder in heaven; and behold a great red dragon, having seven heads and ten horns, and seven crowns upon his heads. ⁴ And his tail drew the third part of the stars of heaven, and did cast them to the earth: and the dragon stood before the woman which was ready to be delivered, for to devour her child as soon as it was born. ⁵ And she brought forth a man child [Jesus], who was to rule all nations with a rod of iron: and her child was caught up unto God, and to his throne. ⁶ And the woman fled into the wilderness [of Jordan, where John the Baptist and Jesus both spent time], where she hath a place prepared of God, that they should feed her there a thousand two hundred and threescore days [3.5 years, or 42 months, or "time, times, and an half" (Daniel 12:7), based on the Jewish lunar calendar].

Revelation 12:1-6

Jesus will gather the Jews just as a Good Shepherd does and bring them from the sheepfold (Bozrah) unto a safe place. Bozrah is in modern Jordan next to the modern town known as Bouseira in Arabic.

¹² I will surely assemble, O Jacob, all of thee; I will surely gather the remnant of Israel; I will put them together as the sheep of Bozrah [Bozrah means "sheepfold"], as the flock in the midst of their fold: they shall make great

noise by reason of the multitude of men. [13] The breaker is come up before them: they have broken up, and have passed through the gate, and are gone out by it: and their king shall pass before them, and the Lord on the head of them.

Micah 2:12-13

Sometime in the Tishri 10 to 15 timeframe, Jesus also will deal directly with the antichrist and his forces. His angels will conduct a second reaping, that of the tares (the wicked) of the parable of the wheat and tares from Matthew 13:24-43, yet this time, the tares are presented as grapes to be crushed.

[17] And another angel came out of the temple which is in heaven, he also having a sharp sickle. [18] And another angel came out from the altar, which had power over fire; and cried with a loud cry to him that had the sharp sickle, saying, Thrust in thy sharp sickle, and gather the clusters of the vine of the earth; for her grapes are fully ripe. [19] And the angel thrust in his sickle into the earth, and gathered the vine of the earth, and cast it into the great winepress of the wrath of God [a reaping that occurs immediately after the reaping of the wheat, i.e., the rapture – rapture followed by wrath, verifying Paul's statement in 1 Thessalonians 5:9 that "God hath not appointed us to wrath"]. [20] And the winepress was trodden without the city, and blood came out of the

winepress, even unto the horse bridles, by the space of a thousand and six hundred furlongs.

Revelation 14:17-20

It is not clear to me if Jesus will gather the Jews being protected in Jordan before the Battle of Armageddon (Revelation 14:17-20 and 16:16) or after, but the language of Micah 2:13 above suggests before, because the Zechariah 12:4-8 passage below says the Jews will participate in the battle.

4 In that day, saith the Lord, I will smite every horse with astonishment, and his rider with madness: and I will open mine eyes upon the house of Judah [in a good way, to their benefit], and will smite every horse of the people [the wicked followers of the antichrist] with blindness. 5 And the governors of Judah shall say in their heart, The inhabitants of Jerusalem shall be my strength in the Lord of hosts their God. 6 In that day will I make the governors of Judah like an hearth of fire among the wood, and like a torch of fire in a sheaf; and they shall devour all the people [the wicked] round about, on the right hand and on the left: and Jerusalem shall be inhabited again in her own place, even in Jerusalem. 7 The Lord also shall save the tents of Judah first, that the glory of the house of David and the glory of the inhabitants of Jerusalem do not magnify themselves against Judah. 8 In that day shall the Lord defend the inhabitants of Jerusalem; and he that

is feeble among them at that day shall be as David; and the house of David shall be as God, as the angel of the Lord before them [meaning the Jews will have great boldness and martial strength].

Zechariah 12:4-8

Jesus will no longer present Himself as the Suffering Servant of Isaiah 53 but will present Himself as the Conquering Warrior of Revelation 19:15-21.

[15] And out of his mouth goeth a sharp sword, that with it he should smite the nations: and he shall rule them with a rod of iron: and he treadeth the winepress [Valley of Megiddo, or Armageddon, a.ka. the valley of decision] of the fierceness and wrath of Almighty God. [16] And he hath on his vesture and on his thigh a name written, King Of Kings, And Lord Of Lords. [17] And I saw an angel standing in the sun; and he cried with a loud voice, saying to all the fowls that fly in the midst of heaven, Come and gather yourselves together unto the supper of the great God [at Armageddon, the valley of decision]; [18] That ye may eat the flesh of kings, and the flesh of captains, and the flesh of mighty men, and the flesh of horses, and of them that sit on them, and the flesh of all men, both free and bond, both small and great. [19] And I saw the beast, and the kings of the earth, and their armies, gathered together to make war against him that

sat on the horse, and against his army. [20] And the beast was taken, and with him the false prophet that wrought miracles before him, with which he deceived them that had received the mark of the beast, and them that worshipped his image. These both were cast alive into a lake of fire burning with brimstone. [21] And the remnant were slain with the sword of him that sat upon the horse, which sword proceeded out of his mouth: and all the fowls were filled with their flesh.

Revelation 19:15-21

Should anyone continue to insist that Jesus is only the meek, mild, Lamb of God who took on the sins of the world, I suggest that they meditate on the following passage indicating that Jesus is also the God of righteous wrath.

[1] Who is this that cometh from Edom, with dyed garments from Bozrah [in Jordan]? this that is glorious in his apparel, travelling in the greatness of his strength? I [Jesus] that speak in righteousness, mighty to save. [2] Wherefore art thou red [refer to His clothes "dipped in blood" in Revelation 19:13] in thine apparel, and thy garments like him that treadeth in the winefat? [3] I [Jesus] have trodden the winepress [the valley of Armageddon, the valley of decision] alone; and of the people [the wicked] there was none with me: for I will tread them in mine anger, and trample them in my fury; and their

blood shall be sprinkled upon my garments, and I will stain all my raiment. ⁴For the day of vengeance is in mine heart, and the year of my redeemed is come. ⁵And I looked, and there was none to help; and I wondered that there was none to uphold: therefore mine own arm brought salvation unto me; and my fury, it upheld me. ⁶And I will tread down the people in mine anger, and make them drunk in my fury, and I will bring down their strength to the earth.

Isaiah 63:1-6

This is a picture of Jesus treading upon the antichrist and his wicked followers in the valley of Armageddon, the valley of decision, the wine press of the fierce wrath of God, in the same manner as one who treads on grapes in a wine press. The details of the demise of the wicked are graphic and not for the faint of heart or the politically correct, but they give an indication of how loathsome and worthy of wrath the followers of the antichrist will be in God's eyes.

¹²And this shall be the plague wherewith the Lord will smite all the people that have fought against Jerusalem; Their flesh shall consume away while they stand upon their feet, and their eyes shall consume away in their holes, and their tongue shall consume away in their mouth.

Zechariah 14:12

After Jesus has vanquished His enemies, His attention will turn to Jerusalem and His future dwelling place, the temple. This brings us to Tishri 15.

Tishri 15 – Tabernacles

[39] Also in the fifteenth day of the seventh month, when ye have gathered in the fruit of the land, ye shall keep a feast unto the Lord seven days: on the first day shall be a sabbath, and on the eighth day shall be a sabbath. [40] And ye shall take you on the first day the boughs of goodly trees, branches of palm trees, and the boughs of thick trees, and willows of the brook; and ye shall rejoice before the Lord your God seven days. [41] And ye shall keep it a feast unto the Lord seven days in the year. It shall be a statute for ever in your generations: ye shall celebrate it in the seventh month. [42] Ye shall dwell in booths seven days; all that are Israelites born shall dwell in booths: [43] That your generations may know that I made the children of Israel to dwell in booths, when I brought them out of the land of Egypt: I am the Lord your God.

Leviticus 23:39-43

The Lord dwelled with the children of Israel as they dwelled in booths, hovering over the tabernacle as a cloud by day and as a pillar of fire by night. The future fulfillment of this OT pattern will conclude with the Lord entering the millennial temple to dwell in the midst of His people Israel for 1,000 years.

> [1] Afterward he brought me to the gate, even the gate that looketh toward the east: [2] And, behold, the glory of the God of Israel came from the way of the east: and his voice was like a noise of many waters: and the earth shined with his glory. [3] And it was according to the appearance of the vision which I saw, even according to the vision that I saw when I came to destroy the city: and the visions were like the vision that I saw by the river Chebar; and I fell upon my face. [4] And the glory of the Lord came into the house by the way of the gate whose prospect is toward the east. [5] So the spirit took me up, and brought me into the inner court; and, behold, the glory of the Lord filled the house. [6] And I heard him speaking unto me out of the house; and the man stood by me. [7] And he said unto me, Son of man, the place of my throne, and the place of the soles of my feet, where I will dwell [tabernacle] in the midst of the children of Israel for ever, and my holy name, shall the house of Israel no more defile, neither they, nor their kings, by their whoredom, nor by the carcases of their kings in their high places.

Ezekiel 43:1-7

But the children of Israel will not be the only people with access to the Lord, for all nations will come to Jerusalem to worship the Lord, and they will forsake war and strife.

> ² And it shall come to pass in the last days, that the mountain of the Lord's house shall be established in the top of the mountains, and shall be exalted above the hills; and all nations shall flow unto it. ³ And many people shall go and say, Come ye, and let us go up to the mountain of the Lord, to the house of the God of Jacob; and he will teach us of his ways, and we will walk in his paths: for out of Zion shall go forth the law, and the word of the Lord from Jerusalem. ⁴ And he shall judge among the nations, and shall rebuke many people: and they shall beat their swords into plowshares, and their spears into pruninghooks: nation shall not lift up sword against nation, neither shall they learn war any more.

Isaiah 2:2-4

This is only scratching the surface of the blessings. Passages from Isaiah 19, Isaiah 65, Ezekiel 47, Joel 2 and 3, Amos 9, and Zechariah 8 tell us that there will be a highway from Egypt to Assyria (Iraq) and that both nations will join with Israel to serve the Lord, thereby reuniting and reconciling Abraham's children, Ishmael (Arabs) and Isaac (Jews); that a child will still be considered young at the age of 100; that a river will flow from the temple for healing the wastelands; that the

Lord will restore the years that the worm has eaten and fill the people's floors and vats with corn, oil, and wine; that the people will experience fully the fruit of their labor; that the lamb will be safe from the wolf, and lions and snakes will be harmless; that the hills and mountains will flow with new wine and milk; that the plowman will overtake the reaper because of the abundance of produce; and that children will play in the streets.

All of this is cause for great hope and expectation. For the believers living at the time of the antichrist's reign, these promised pleasures and joys should bring great hope and encouragement to endure to the end. The pains of the antichrist will be short-lived, yet the pleasures of God will endure forever. And the ultimate pleasure will be in our midst.

[11] Thou wilt shew me the path of life: in thy presence is fulness of joy; **at thy right hand there are pleasures for evermore**.

Psalm 16:11

And Who sits at the right hand of the Father? Jesus. May He come quickly.

[20] He which testifieth these things saith, Surely I come quickly. Amen. Even so, come, Lord Jesus.

Revelation 22:20

CPSIA information can be obtained
at www.ICGtesting.com
Printed in the USA
BVHW060811040720
582849BV00007B/21